Clear**Revise**

AQA GCSE
Design and Technology 8552

Illustrated revision and practice

Published by
PG Online Limited
The Old Coach House
35 Main Road
Tolpuddle
Dorset
DT2 7EW
United Kingdom

sales@pgonline.co.uk
www.clearrevise.com
www.pgonline.co.uk
2020

PG ONLINE

PREFACE

Absolute clarity! That's the aim.

This is everything you need to ace your exam and beam with pride. Each topic is laid out in a beautifully illustrated format that is clear, approachable and as concise and simple as possible.

Each section of the specification is clearly indicated to help you cross-reference your revision. The checklist on the contents pages will help you keep track of what you have already worked through and what's left before the big day.

We have included worked exam-style questions with answers for almost every topic. This helps you understand where marks are awarded and to see the theory at work for yourself in an examination situation. There is also a set of exam-style questions at the end of each section for you to practise writing answers for. You can check your answers against those given at the end of the book.

LEVELS OF LEARNING

Based on the degree to which you are able to truly understand a new topic, we recommend that you work in stages. Start by reading a short explanation of something, then try and recall what you've just read. This has limited effect if you stop there but it aids the next stage. Question everything. Write down your own summary and then complete and mark a related exam-style question. Cover up the answers if necessary, but learn from them once you've seen them. Lastly, teach someone else. Explain the topic in a way that they can understand. Have a go at the different practice questions – they offer an insight into how and where marks are awarded.

Design and artwork: Mike Bloys & Jessica Webb / PG Online Ltd
First edition 2020. 10 9 8 7 6 5 4 3 2

A catalogue entry for this book is available from the British Library
ISBN: 978-1-910523-24-7
Copyright © L Sheppard 2020
All rights reserved

MIX
Paper from
responsible sources
FSC® C007785

THE SCIENCE OF REVISION

Illustrations and words

Research has shown that revising with words and pictures doubles the quality of responses by students.[1] This is known as 'dual-coding' because it provides two ways of fetching the information from our brain. The improvement in responses is particularly apparent in students when asked to apply their knowledge to different problems. Recall, application and judgement are all specifically and carefully assessed in public examination questions.

Retrieval of information

Retrieval practice encourages students to come up with answers to questions.[2] The closer the question is to one you might see in a real examination, the better. Also, the closer the environment in which a student revises is to the 'examination environment', the better. Students who had a test 2–7 days away did 30% better using retrieval practice than students who simply read, or repeatedly reread material. Students who were expected to teach the content to someone else after their revision period did better still.[3] What was found to be most interesting in other studies is that students using retrieval methods and testing for revision were also more resilient to the introduction of stress.[4]

Ebbinghaus' forgetting curve and spaced learning

Ebbinghaus' 140-year-old study examined the rate in which we forget things over time. The findings still hold power. However, the act of forgetting things and relearning them is what cements things into the brain.[5] Spacing out revision is more effective than cramming – we know that, but students should also know that the space between revisiting material should vary depending on how far away the examination is. A cyclical approach is required. An examination 12 months away necessitates revisiting covered material about once a month. A test in 30 days should have topics revisited every 3 days – intervals of roughly a tenth of the time available.[6]

Summary

Students: the more tests and past questions you do, in an environment as close to examination conditions as possible, the better you are likely to perform on the day. If you prefer to listen to music while you revise, tunes without lyrics will be far less detrimental to your memory and retention. Silence is most effective.[5] If you choose to study with friends, choose carefully – effort is contagious.[7]

1. Mayer, R. E., & Anderson, R. B. (1991). Animations need narrations: An experimental test of dual-coding hypothesis. *Journal of Education Psychology*, (83)4, 484-490.

2. Roediger III, H. L., & Karpicke, J.D. (2006). Test-enhanced learning: Taking memory tests improves long-term retention. *Psychological Science*, 17(3), 249-255.

3. Nestojko, J., Bui, D., Kornell, N. & Bjork, E. (2014). Expecting to teach enhances learning and organisation of knowledge in free recall of text passages. *Memory and Cognition*, 42(7), 1038-1048.

4. Smith, A. M., Floerke, V. A., & Thomas, A. K. (2016) Retrieval practice protects memory against acute stress. *Science*, 354(6315), 1046-1048.

5. Perham, N., & Currie, H. (2014). Does listening to preferred music improve comprehension performance? *Applied Cognitive Psychology*, 28(2), 279-284.

6. Cepeda, N. J., Vul, E., Rohrer, D., Wixted, J. T. & Pashler, H. (2008). Spacing effects in learning a temporal ridgeline of optimal retention. *Psychological Science*, 19(11), 1095-1102.

7. Busch, B. & Watson, E. (2019), *The Science of Learning*, 1st ed. Routledge.

CONTENTS

Section A Core technical principles

3.1.1 New and emerging technologies ☑

3.1.2 Energy Generation and storage ☑

3.1.3 Development in new materials ☑

3.1.4 Systems approach to designing ☑

3.1.5 Mechanical devices ☑

3.1.6 Materials and their working properties ☑

Section B Specialist technical principles

3.2.1 Selection of materials or components ☑

3.2.2 Forces and stresses ☑

3.2.3 Ecological and social footprint ☑

Papers and boards ☑

Timbers

☑

Metals

☑

Polymers

☑

Textiles

☑

Electronics and mechanical systems

☑

3.2.7 Scales of production

☑

3.2.8 Specialist techniques and processes

☑

Section C Designing and making principles

Designing principles

☑

Making principles

☑

MARK ALLOCATIONS

Green mark allocations[1] on answers to in-text questions through this guide help to indicate where marks are gained within the answers. A bracketed '1' e.g. [1] = one valid point worthy of a mark. There are often alternative responses with many more points to make than there are marks available so you have more opportunity to max out your answers than you may think.

ACKNOWLEDGEMENTS

The questions in the ClearRevise textbook are the sole responsibility of the authors and have neither been provided nor approved by the examination board.

Every effort has been made to trace and acknowledge ownership of copyright. The publishers will be happy to make any future amendments with copyright owners that it has not been possible to contact. The author and publisher would like to thank the following companies and individuals who granted permission for the use of their images in this textbook.

Social media logos © tanuha2001 / Shutterstock.com
Fairtrade Logo © The Fairtrade Foundation
Stacked paperback books © Imfoto / Shutterstock.com
Underground map © ChrisDorney / Shutterstock.com
Reichstag dome © Kapi Ng / Shutterstock.com
Mini Cooper car © JazzBoo / Shutterstock.com
McQueen catwalk © FashionStock.com / Shutterstock.com
Marigold print © RawPixel.com / Shutterstock.com
Mary Quant stamp © Neftali / Shutterstock.com
St Cataldo cemetery © AJ165 / Shutterstock.com
Rietveld chair © Picture Partners / Shutterstock.com
Rennie Mackintosh dressing table © Derek Harris Photography / Shutterstock.com
Orange juicer © CKP1001 / Shutterstock.com
Westwood catwalk © Taniavolobueva / Shutterstock.com

Apple Watch © Alexey Boldin / Shutterstock.com
Gap store © Testing / Shutterstock.com
Primark store © Stanislav Samoylik / Shutterstock.com
Under Armour store © BT Image / Shutterstock.com
Zara store © Testing / Shutterstock.com
Polymorph © Mindsets Online
Tamper proof sticker © StickerYou Inc
Maun ruler © Maun Industries Ltd
Coco Chanel © Getty Images
Sottsass © Getty Images
Templier © Getty Images
Alessi © Alessi S.p.a
Dyson Supersonic TM © Dyson Ltd
Engineers Blue © ICS Industrial
FSC logo © Forest Stewardship Council

SECTION A
3.1 Core technical principles

Information

At least 15% of the exam will assess maths and at least 10% will assess science.

All dimensions are in millimetres.

The marks for questions are shown in brackets.

The maximum mark for this paper is 100.

The qualification is subject to the assessment of one NEA project and one examination.

There are 20 marks for Section A, 30 marks for Section B and 50 marks for Section C.

NEW AND EMERGING TECHNOLOGIES

Technology impacts our lives in many ways and is being developed to improve how we live and work.

Design technologists have always looked to the world of science in order to utilise new discoveries in the design and manufacture of materials or products. In harnessing these new discoveries, technology continues to develop and meet ongoing human needs.

Technology utilises many skills including communication, design, innovation, modelling and manufacturing. It also combines knowledge, problem solving and organised, structured methods to produce finished items. Designers and manufacturers use a combination of skilled people, tools, robots and machines for efficient and effective output of their product or service.

Consumers are continually looking for new and improved products, which means manufacturers are developing more and more items to satisfy demand. It is critical to understand the impact design and technology has on the world.

The collection of raw materials and converting them into usable products can use vast amounts of energy, which is having a negative impact on the planet. Designers are continually exploring new methods of working with technology to manufacture products more sustainably. These continuous improvements lead to greater efficiencies, improved functionality, which in turn reduces energy output and negative effects on the environment.

INDUSTRY

Designers utilise technology to continually improve the efficiency and quality in manufacturing products and materials.

Automation and the use of robotics

Automation enables repetitive tasks to be performed by mechanised assembly lines rather than by a human. It has been a significant development in the manufacturing process and helps meet increased demand for products. Software automation performs computer-based tasks, industrial automation performs physical tasks.

Robots can be controlled to automatically perform a series of complex movements. They can be used to substitute humans in environments that are hazardous, exposed to high temperatures or where there are harmful vapours. They are commonly used on assembly lines in the manufacture of vehicles, in packing plants, laboratories and in aerospace.

Advantages

- Increased efficiency and speed of production
- Accurate and consistent output
- Reduced labour costs and can work 24/7
- Ability to work in a variety of environments

Disadvantages

- Replaces workforce leading to some job losses
- No human input/decision making
- Up-skilled workforce to maintain robots
- Expensive to set up

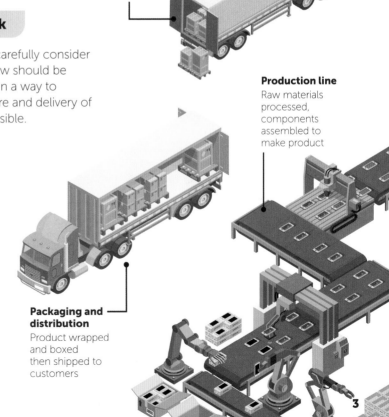

Delivery depot
Raw materials/
components

Production line
Raw materials processed, components assembled to make product

Packaging and distribution
Product wrapped and boxed then shipped to customers

Buildings and the place of work

At the point of conception, companies carefully consider the layout of their buildings. The workflow should be logically thought through and designed in a way to ensure each stage of design, manufacture and delivery of a product to market is as efficient as possible.

> Describe **two** factors that make the production of circuit boards suitable for automated assembly line manufacture. [4]
>
> *Identical circuit boards and products are passed through the production line[1] making it easy to program robots to perform repetitive operations[1]. Precision is required and must be maintained[1] robots are able to work consistently and indefinitely[1].*

ENTERPRISE

Enterprise is the ability to identify a business opportunity, develop it and make it commercially successful. A start-up company is usually one that has come up with an idea that has the potential to grow into a profit-making business.

By applying for a patent, original ideas, discoveries and inventions remain the **intellectual property** of the person who invented them. This is a legal process of proving the creator is the first person to have registered the idea or invention.

Crowd funding is the use of small amounts of capital from many individuals to finance a new business venture. The use of websites and social media enables a broad range of investors from individuals to venture capitalists to invest in an idea, usually in return for shares should the venture succeed. It provides a new platform for businesses to reach a large audience of funders and is an alternative to the traditional route of a bank loan. However if the venture doesn't reach a funding target, any finance pledged is usually returned to investors. If the project fails it can damage the reputation of the company.

Virtual marketing and **virtual retail** include the use of websites, social media, email and digital marketing to reach a wider audience and potential client base in order to promote a product, service or idea. Virtual marketing relies on hits, clicks or likes. The effect of this can be measured more easily than with print advertising. Virtual marketing also includes paid-for advertisements in search results.

A **cooperative** is an enterprise that is commonly owned and run by its members who may comprise its workforce or its customers. Cooperatives are formed to enable a group of people with the same business interests to have greater protection and a stronger democratic voice.

Fair trade is about better prices, decent working conditions and fair terms of trade for farmers and workers in less economically developed countries. The Fairtrade Foundation requires companies pay a fair and sustainable price for their produce, enabling farmers to improve their quality of life. The Fairtrade Foundation focus on products exported from developing countries to developed countries such as fruit, coffee, chocolate, wine and cotton.

A new plant-based food manufacturer is using social media to raise awareness of its crowd funding campaign.

(a) Give **two** advantages of using social media to raise awareness for the new company. [2]

(b) Explain **one** disadvantage of crowd funding to the new company. [2]

(a) *Social media enables mass-marketing for low cost.[1] It can attract global attention[1], making use of text, graphics and video to achieve a viral advertising campaign[1].*

(b) *If crowd funding doesn't reach its funding target, the money invested so far may have to be returned, affecting the project as a whole and the reputation of the manufacturer.[1]*

SUSTAINABILITY

Sustainability looks to protect and maintain the needs of the present without compromising the ability of future generations to meet their needs.

Designers now have a better understanding of which materials are sustainable, which are not, and the effect that overharvesting and overconsumption has on the planet.

Finite resources

Finite resources are in limited supply and are being used more quickly than can be replaced. Use of finite resources should be avoided where possible or used only in small amounts for essential reasons where an alternative cannot be used. Fossil fuels, some minerals and metal ores are examples of finite resources.

Non-finite resources

Non-finite resources are in abundant supply and are unlikely ever to be exhausted. They can be grown or replaced at the rate that they are being used. Examples include solar and wind energy, timbers and cotton.

Life Cycle Assessment

Conducting a **Life Cycle Assessment** (**LCA**) is a way for companies to assess the environmental impact of a product during the different stages of a product's life.

1. Extraction and processing: The amount of energy used to extract raw material from the earth, or to produce it through farming or other methods, and process it ready for manufacturing.

2. Manufacturing and production: The energy required to manipulate the raw and refined materials into a product ready for sale.

Life Cycle Assessment (LCA)

5. End of life

3. Distribution: The packaging and transportation of the product to the end user.

4. Use

Waste disposal

Careful planning of **waste disposal** has many positive effects, particularly in large scale manufacturing plants. Waste materials can be reused internally for alternative parts and products. Some of the cost of materials is recouped through the sale of recyclable waste. The energy used to heat and power a business may also be generated from waste material such as biomass.

Plastic straws have been phased out from use in many national restaurant chains.

Explain the benefits of replacing these with paper straws. [2]

Biodegradable / paper straws decompose more quickly[1], reducing waste in landfill[1]. They are manufactured with fewer finite resources[1].

ENVIRONMENT

Humans place a demand on the earth's natural resources in order to develop a modern lifestyle. An accelerated use of Earth's natural resources means they are being used up at an unsustainable rate. New technologies and designs are being adopted to reduce the negative impact on the environment.

Global warming

Manufacturing and the burning of fossil fuels contributes to increased levels of carbon dioxide (CO_2) and other air pollutants that are collecting in the atmosphere. This contributes to global warming which is increasing the average global temperature and causing extreme weather events.

Pollution

Pollution introduces harmful materials into the environment. Manufacturing generates pollution by burning fossil fuels for energy and transportation. As well as air pollution it may also contaminate water and land or create noise and light pollution. Businesses have several options to reduce the levels of pollution caused by the manufacture of a product. By conducting a **Life Cycle Assessment** (**LCA**), a company will find out how much pollution is being created and plan a reduction strategy.

Continuous improvement

Many manufacturers make small but continuous improvements to their processes and workflow. They adopt a strategy within the workplace to make regular improvements that may be small incremental changes or adjustments to bigger processes. Companies that focus on continual improvement become more efficient and more effective.

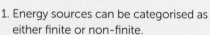

1. Energy sources can be categorised as either finite or non-finite.

   (a) State what is meant by a
       non-finite resource. [1]

   (b) Give **one** example of a finite
       energy source. [1]

       *(a) A resource that is found naturally
       and can be replaced.[1]*

       *(b) Fossil fuels such as coal[1], crude
       oil[1] and natural gas.[1]*

PEOPLE

Designers and manufacturers need to understand the marketplace when launching a new product successfully.

People across the world can have very different needs and tastes, and products successfully launched in one country can be a complete failure in another.

The Internet has helped create a global marketplace and increased competition which gives the consumer access to greater choice and lower prices.

Technology push

When new technology becomes available, designers will utilise it to make a product before the market is aware of it. Research and development teams will introduce new technology, manufacturing processes and materials to push through the design of new products or improve existing ones. This will often make them smaller, cheaper or more efficient.

Market pull

When the market needs a product, designers will make something to meet that demand. This will be in response to market forces and customer needs. Examples include recyclable carrier bags, low energy lamps and gluten free foods.

Changing job roles

Technology in the workplace is continually changing. Automation commonly leads to a reduction of manual labour or a change in job roles and working conditions. The workforce can be retrained for new positions using new technologies, often giving people new and higher value skills.

Efficient working

Methods to improve efficiency and productivity are adopted by businesses to reduce costs, energy usage and impact on the environment. Companies will invest in staff training, and improved working practises for the workforce. The use of new technologies, automation and reduction of wastage all contribute to company efficiencies.

2. Explain **one** benefit to the environment of using non-finite energy resources. [2]

Non-finite resources are either in limitless supply or they are easily replaced[1] which means we are not using up natural resources that are in limited supply[1]. Harnessing renewable energy is less detrimental to the environment than extracting finite materials[1], for example, drilling for oil, or mining coal can disrupt surrounding eco systems[1]. Renewable energy generates electricity which can be cleanly consumed.[1] fossil fuels can cause pollution.[1]

CULTURE

Culture is an amalgamation of the ideas, beliefs, customs and social behaviours of a society or group of people. It often manifests itself through ritual, art and fashion. It is important for designers to be aware of the society around them and to try to understand the different cultures that exist within it.

Fashion and trends

Fashion and trends come and go. The design market is influenced by the 'latest thing'. It is quite natural for consumers to want to buy into a certain lifestyle. Blog sites, social media and the Internet enable new fashion and products to be showcased or endorsed. They can receive a very rapid customer response.

Faiths and beliefs

A designer must be responsible for considering the wider implications of a new product within different faiths and communities and in meeting the needs of different groups of society.

Discuss how clothing designs, fabric colour and materials may sell well in one country but not in another. [3]

Faiths and beliefs restrict the styles of clothing that some people wear.[1] A popular style of top or shorts exposing the shoulders or knees is considered too revealing in some areas of the world.[1] Green is considered a positive, environmentally friendly colour in the West, and is the traditional colour of Islam. In Indonesia, green has traditionally been forbidden.[1] White symbolises purity and cleanliness in Western cultures. However, in China and Korea, white represents death and bad luck.[1] Silks may sell very well in Asian cultures, as part of national dress styles, but less so in the West.[1]

SOCIETY

Design for differently abled and elderly

Products are often designed for the average user. **Inclusive design** is important for any new product to ensure the environment or design can be used by as many people as possible, regardless of gender, disability or age. All users should be able to use the design safely, easily and with dignity.

Designers will consider these factors when working on a new product, improving access to buildings, or looking at how people access different types of transport. Modern materials have enabled products to be lighter, tougher and more adaptable to help with weaker grip, and reduced mobility.

A charitable organisation inspects and awards new car parks with a rating for their accessibility and facilities.

Describe how car park design can incorporate features to improve accessibility for all users including the disabled and the elderly. [3]

Clear and visible signage to identify entrances, exits, walkways.[1] The height of payment machines, lift buttons, exit panels[1] are considered so that wheelchair users can reach easily[1]. Lifts as well as stairs to assist those who find stairs difficult.[1] Handrails and balustrades on stairwells.[1] Automatic opening doors with sensors.[1] Wide parking bays for disabled vehicular access and those with push chairs[1]. Well lit walkways.[1] Induction loop systems and assistive listening in payment, information and lift spaces.[1]

PRODUCTION TECHNIQUES AND SYSTEMS

Manufacturing methods

A **flexible manufacturing system** (**FMS**) is a method of production designed to easily adapt to changes in the quantity or type of product being manufactured.

Systems can be configured to manage any change in levels of production and make parts that are appropriate. A manufacturer may implement FMS to manage their stock inventory and production planning system. By having an item tracking system, every part in the warehouse can be easily traced and monitored. A good production plan will identify the times and deadlines for each process such as accessing parts from the warehouse, machining, assembly and packing times.

Lean manufacturing focuses on minimising waste and improving efficiency, which in turn is cost saving and reduces the use of resources. The elimination of waste is core to a lean practise.

FotoPrint allows customers to design their own books containing their favourite photos and memories. Once a book has been designed, FotoPrint will print, bind and send copies to the customer.

Explain how a flexible manufacturing system would be an advantage to FotoPrint.   [2]

Automated machines are used[1] that can be reprogrammed / recalibrated / retooled easily between production runs[1] to adjust for print volume[1], hard or soft covers, book dimensions[1], finish[1] and paper type[1].

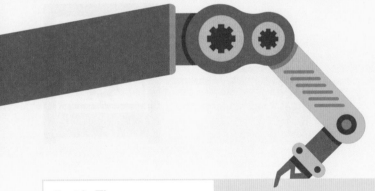

Just in Time
Manufacturers use the Just-in-Time (JIT) production method to respond to customer demand. By closely monitoring stock, products can be reordered as needed.

Advantages

- Products are made to order, saving on storage space.
- Stock doesn't become old or out of date.
- More factory space can be utilised for other activities.
- Materials and components are ordered as needed, keeping cash flow in control.

Disadvantages

- The supply chain must be reliable and fast.
- Sales are affected by any delay in deliveries or product failures.
- Costs are higher, ordering in small quantities prevents bulk volume discounts.

CAD AND CAM

Computer aided design

Computer aided design (**CAD**) enables designers, engineers and architects to produce precise technical drawings using a computer. It can be used to create 2D drawings or 3D models.

Designers can edit and amend designs more easily, create revisions and change aspects such as scale, colour or texture with ease. CAD is important for visualisation before manufacture, as it conveys an idea with clarity which can improve workflow and efficiency, and in some cases save money.

Advantages

- Accurate designs.
- Changes and corrections can be easily made.
- Software can automate some design tasks.
- Designs can be shared and viewed simultaneously.
- Designs can be rendered to simulate the final finish.
- 3D models can be produced from the designs.

Disadvantages

- Cost of software, hi-spec computer and printer.
- Work maybe lost, data corrupted or hacked.
- Time taken to learn complex software.

Computer aided manufacture

CAM uses computer software to control machine tools and machinery in the manufacturing process. It helps streamline production by translating CAD data into an instruction for a piece of machinery or tooling such as a laser cutter or CNC mill. It increases productivity, is highly accurate and consistent, resulting in reduced waste.

Ethics

Designers should research how the use of new materials is likely to impact the environment by conducting a **life cycle assessment** (**LCA**). Companies are increasing their environmental and social credentials, due to consumer demand and are considering their ecological footprint in the manufacturing process. Manufactures may consider unethical solutions to cutting production costs including the use of low or underpaid labour, compromising safety factors or illegal waste disposal.

The **Waste Electrical and Electronic Equipment** (**WEEE**) regulations require UK businesses to:

- Minimise waste from their electrical equipment and promote reuse.
- Ensure waste products are recycled correctly and meet material recovery targets.
- Design products by reducing material use and enhancing reusability and recyclability.

HOW THE EVALUATION OF NEW AND EMERGING TECHNOLOGIES INFORMS DESIGN DECISIONS

Planned or built-in obsolescence

A product is designed to perform its task for an appropriate period of time. Planned obsolescence is a deliberate strategy to ensure that a current version of a product will become out of date or worn out within a given time frame. In the technology sector this may mean that the software becomes incompatible, there is insufficient processor power or components wear out. The lifespan of a product can also be affected by trends and customer demand. Manufacturers may design a product to maintain regular sales.

Environment

Designers should encompass end-of-life systems, takeback programmes, recovery and recycling as part of their planning. The treatment or disposal of materials once they have reached their end-of-life is an important step. This should be managed efficiently to minimise carbon emissions and the use of landfill.

Design for maintenance

When a product is designed for maintenance, it enables parts that have worn out or broken to be replaced. Repairing is positive for the environment as it saves the whole product from being thrown away, creates employment for engineers and a spare parts supply chain.

A product's lifespan can be improved by making it easier to repair and recycle.

(a) Give **one** design feature that makes a product easier to repair at home. [1]

(b) Give **two** ways a company can design a product to improve its recyclability. [2]

(a) Using regular fixings that can be accessed using non-specialist tools.[1] Design products so that they can be easily disassembled.[1]

(b) Using as few materials as possible.[1] Using recyclable materials.[1] Making different materials easy to separate from each other by avoiding permanent bonding methods.[1]

Design for disassembly

The design process is continually being assessed to address the selection of materials, so that at 'end of life' a product can be disassembled, and components and materials can be recycled or reused.

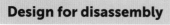

| Cost | Reliability | Longevity | Sustainability | Recyclability |

EXAMINATION PRACTICE

1. Explain **one** advantage of the use of robotics in the workplace. [2]

2. Give **two** reasons why workplace buildings should be laid out efficiently. [2]

3. Give **two** examples of products that could be supplied as fair trade items. [2]

4. Give **two** different communication methods that would be classified as a form of virtual marketing. [2]

5. Which **one** of the following is a finite energy source? [1]
   (a) Solar
   (b) Oil
   (c) Tidal
   (d) Wind

6. State what is meant by a non-finite resource. [1]

7. Burning fossil fuels releases carbon dioxide into the earth's atmosphere which is linked to global warming.
   Give **two** effects of global warming. [2]

8. Describe **two** ways in which companies can dispose of their waste without having to send it to landfill. [2]

9. Explain what is meant by each of the following terms: [4]
   • Technology push
   • Market pull

10. A company is planning to raise funds for their new business by crowd funding and a bank loan in the ratio of 5:2 respectively.
    They want to raise £14 million.
    Calculate how much money they would raise from crowd funding. [2]

11. Give **three** benefits of using computer aided design (CAD) rather than traditional hand drawing. [3]

12. Explain **two** advantages to the manufacturer of using Just in Time (JIT) as a production technique. [2]

13. Explain why manufacturers produce products with built in obsolescence. [2]

14. Explain why products are becoming more difficult or expensive to repair. [2]

ENERGY GENERATION

How we generate and store energy has a global impact on our lives. We are very dependent on electricity and much of this is produced by burning fossil fuels. The use of renewable energy sources is increasing. Energy generation can be separated into two main categories, fossil fuels and renewables.

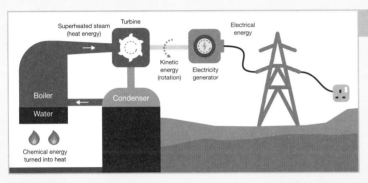

Turbines and generators

Production of electricity involves rotating a turbine which turns a generator. **Fossil fuels** are commonly **burned** to create heat which **superheats water**. The resultant **steam** rotates the **turbine** which is linked to a **generator** to produce electricity.

Fossil fuels

Fossil fuels are finite resources. Natural **gas** is a main source of power for electricity in the UK. It's also used for heating and cooking. **Coal** is burned to create energy. **Oil** is mainly used to produce plastics or for fuel. Burning these fuels produces large amounts of carbon dioxide which contributes to climate change.

Advantages

- A cheap and reliable source of energy, well developed systems to harness the energy.

Disadvantages

- Contains high amounts of carbon and contributes to global warming.
- A non-renewable and unsustainable energy source.
- Accidents such as oil spills contribute to pollution and environmental contamination.

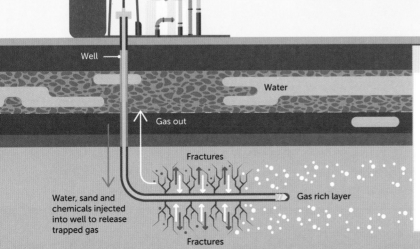

Shale gas

Shale gas is a natural gas trapped in the earth's crust. Hydraulic fracturing or '**fracking**' is a process for extracting the gas from the shale, by sending a high pressure mixture of water, sand and chemicals into the rock to release the gas.

NUCLEAR POWER

A nuclear power plant produces energy through a process called fission - the splitting of uranium atoms in a nuclear reactor.

The process harnesses a nuclear reaction which takes place inside a reactor. This releases a large amount of energy as heat. The heat is used to generate steam which drives turbines to produce electricity.

Nuclear power is clean and efficient. Nuclear energy runs continuously generating large scale power and supplies about 12% of the world's electricity. However, the waste material is radioactive and dangerous to life. The waste fuel requires specialist handling, decommissioning and lots of storage space.

Wind energy and fossil fuel energy are both used to create power. Explain the similarities and differences between their methods of power generation. [3]

Fossil fuels are burnt to heat water.[1] The resulting steam turns turbines[1], which turn generators[1]. Wind directly turns a turbine which turns generators.[1] Generators supply electricity to the National Grid.

RENEWABLE ENERGY

Wind, wave, tidal, hydroelectric, geothermal, biomass and solar energy are renewable. These are natural sources of energy that are **non-finite** and can be quickly replenished.

Wind power

Wind turbines convert kinetic energy from the wind into electricity. The energy of the wind turns the propeller-like blades on the rotor. This is connected to a generator which creates the electricity.

Advantages

Wind energy is now very cost effective to produce. It is a clean source of energy and is sustainable and renewable.

Disadvantages

Wind energy can be unpredictable and wind farms affect the visual appearance of the landscape. The distance from remote wind sites and connection costs to the national grid may be significant.

Tidal power

Tidal power converts energy from tides into power. The movement of water turns underwater turbines, which drive the generators that convert the energy into electricity. Tidal barrage systems utilise the difference between low and high tides. Tidal stream power utilises fast flowing currents around coasts and islands.

Advantages

A constant, predictable, renewable energy source which is clean.

Disadvantages

Expensive to set up and maintain.

Solar panels

Solar panels absorb light into **photovoltaic cells** which is converted into electricity.

Advantages

Renewable, clean power, no greenhouse gases. Energy can be collected on sunny or cloudy days.

Disadvantages

Energy generation levels are lower in winter months when daylight hours are shorter, compared to production in summer months when daylight hours are longer.

Biomass energy

Biomass energy is produced from organic matter such as plants, crops, wood chips and animal waste. The energy can be extracted by burning or anaerobic digestion, which creates a biogas and a biofertiliser.

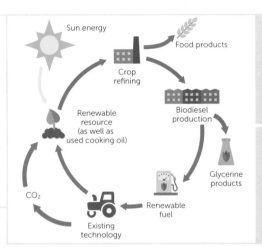

Advantages

A renewable form of energy with a plentiful supply of material. Carbon neutral.

Disadvantages

Risk of deforestation if trees are not replanted. Increase in CO_2 emissions.

Hydroelectric power

Hydroelectric power (**HEP**) captures the energy of falling water. A turbine converts this **kinetic energy** into mechanical energy, and a generator turns this to electricity. Dams are the most common structures used for harnessing hydroelectric power. See **kinetic pumped storage systems** on page 16.

Advantages

Hydroelectric energy is renewable, reliable and does not pollute. It can be regulated according to demand.

Disadvantages

The cost and environmental pollution of dam construction is very high. The local environment is affected by flooding of a valley, which impacts on surrounding water flow. This in turn affects natural irrigation and ecosystems.

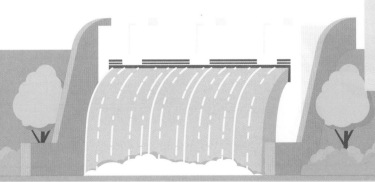

ENERGY STORAGE

Different technologies are used to store energy, so it can be used on demand or stored for use at a later time. Storage can be in many forms and sizes depending on the power supply needed for a system. These include pumped storage systems, batteries, flywheels and capacitors.

Kinetic energy

Kinetic energy is the energy an object has because of its motion. Hydroelectric facilities harness the powerful force of gravity to enable this form of energy storage. The facilities comprise of two reservoirs and a hydroelectric dam system.

Kinetic pumped storage systems are used to efficiently manage a supply of energy and rapidly top up the National Grid electricity supply at peak times. A hydroelectric storage facility holds water in an upper reservoir. At times of high electricity demand, the dam is opened and the water released into a lower reservoir to drive the turbines, producing electricity. At times of low electricity demand, such as at night, the water is pumped back up to the upper reservoir ready for the cycle to continue.

Batteries contain chemicals that are toxic and should be disposed of correctly at a recycling centre. If batteries end up in landfill, the chemicals can contaminate the ground causing soil or water pollution, harming the environment.

A wall mounted clock requires four 1.5-volt batteries to work.

Calculate how many rechargeable batteries would be required if used instead. [2]

The clock will need five 1.2 volt[1] batteries to work.

Batteries

Batteries contain electro-chemicals that react with each other to produce an electric voltage.

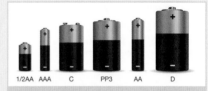

1/2AA   AAA   C   PP3   AA   D

Alkaline battery
Alkaline batteries have a high energy capacity and long shelf life. Once the chemical reactants have been used, the battery is flat and no longer usable. The power output gradually decreases.

A typical battery holds 1.5 volts per cell.

Rechargeable battery
Rechargeable batteries can be charged many times. The energy to charge a battery comes from mains electricity. The power output remains constant until they run flat. Available in different types for higher powered uses.

A typical rechargeable battery holds 1.2 volts per cell.

MODERN MATERIALS

Designers are always seeking ways to improve the performance of materials. In developing new materials or improving the use of existing materials, new products and applications can be developed.

Graphene

Graphene is a single layer of carbon atoms, tightly bound in a hexagonal lattice. It is the thinnest known material to date, extremely strong, light and conductive to heat and electricity. Used in sports equipment, cooling technology in mobile phones, batteries, solar applications, aerospace and more.

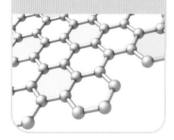

Metal foam

Metal foams are a cellular structure made up from metal containing gas filled pores. With good stiffness to weight ratio, they are strong, resist deformation and can be made into complex geometrical forms. Foams have good heat resistance and sound absorption. Used for weight saving and impact absorbing structures in vehicles.

Liquid crystal display

Low-power LCD displays such as televisions, contain a matrix of pixels that display an image on the screen. A backlight provides light to the individual pixels. By varying the levels of red, green and blue light, millions of colour combinations are created and displayed.

Coated metals

Metal coatings help protect metal, make it more durable and reduce wear and tear. An unprotected ferrous metal is liable to rust and corrosion due to exposure to the environment. Examples include galvanised steel, plastic coatings such as Teflon, anodising, thermoplastic dip coating and painting.

Titanium

Found in the earth's crust, Titanium is used in the form of an alloy. It has high strength, is lightweight and resists corrosion. These properties make it suitable for use in missiles, space and aircraft. It does not react with human tissue so is used in medicine for artificial joints.

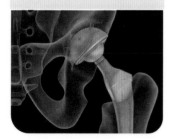

Nanomaterials

Nanomaterials are materials or substances made at a very small scale. These natural or manufactured materials contain particles less than 100 nanometres in size. Nanotechnology adds properties to products, such as lightness, tensile strength and rigidity. These are being used in electronics and the world of medicine. Nanotechnology is able to incorporate useful properties into textiles which can make them resistant to bacteria, super hydrophobic (water repellent), repel dirt and neutralise bad odours.

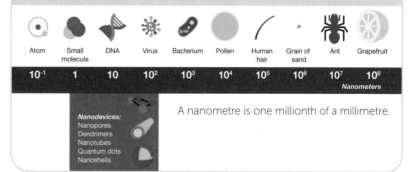

Atom	Small molecule	DNA	Virus	Bacterium	Pollen	Human hair	Grain of sand	Ant	Grapefruit
10^{-1}	1	10	10^2	10^3	10^4	10^5	10^6	10^7	10^8

Nanometers

Nanodevices:
Nanopores
Dendrimers
Nanotubes
Quantum dots
Nanoshells

A nanometre is one millionth of a millimetre.

SMART MATERIALS

Smart materials are responsive materials that are designed to react to external stimuli. They can alter the functional or aesthetic properties in response to a changing environment.

Polymorph

Polymorph is a polymer that can be shaped and reshaped many times. When warmed to 62°C, the polymorph becomes flexible and easy to mould into the desired shape. It sets as it cools and becomes stiff and strong. It can be used for making bespoke shapes such as ergonomic handles, is useful for making prototype mechanical parts and for making mouldings.

Shape memory alloy (SMA)

Shape memory alloys are a group of materials that revert back to their original shape after being deformed by heat or another external stimulus. Nitinol is an SMA with shape memory properties. It is used in dentistry for braces, for activating a variable resistor or switch when there is a fluctuation in temperature, frames for spectacles and self-bending spoons in magic shows. Given its thermal shape memory and super-elasticity, Nitinol mesh is used for expandable stents in vascular surgery, for treating blocked arteries.

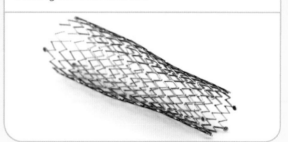

Quantum tunnelling composite (QTC)

Quantum tunnelling composite is a flexible polymer with tiny metal particles embedded into it. When the material is squeezed, pressure forces the particles together and a current of electrons flows between the neighbouring particles. The process of electrons jumping across a gap from one conducting material to another is known as quantum tunnelling. It is used in microswitches, outdoor items that may be affected by water and touch sensitive pads.

A motorcycle helmet manufacturer is considering the use of photochromic pigments on its visors.

Explain **one** disadvantage of using photochromic particles with helmet visors. [2]

They take up to two minutes to darken or lighten[1], which can cause issues when entering tunnels or shady areas or going straight out into bright sunlight[1]. They can lose their ability to turn back to clear over time[1], which means they become less effective in different light levels[1].

Thermochromic materials

Thermochromic materials are temperature sensitive. They change colour at certain ranges of temperature, be it cold activations, rub and reveal or hot applications. They can be incorporated into inks and printed onto plastic in the form of temperature indicators.

Photochromic materials

Photochromic pigments change colour when exposed to different UV levels. In the example of glasses, the lens may darken when exposed to bright sunlight and reverse to colourless once removed from the UV source. The pigments are also used in textile printing inks and novelty toys. Over time the pigments degrade from over exposure to UV light.

COMPOSITE MATERIALS

A composite material is composed of at least two materials. When combined, the properties are superior to those of the individual components.

Glass reinforced plastic (GRP)

Glass reinforced plastic is a polyester material reinforced with the addition of glass fibre. It is produced by combining thermosetting polyester resin and glass fibre matting making a strong and lightweight composite. GRP is used in the manufacture of circuit boards, in the marine industry for boat hulls and in the custom kit car market.

Carbon fibre reinforced plastic (CRP)

Carbon fibre reinforced plastic is a thermoplastic reinforced with carbon fibres. It has a high strength to weight ratio and is very rigid. It is used in aerospace engineering for fuselage components, Formula One vehicle chassis and many items of sports equipment including running blades used by para-athletes.

> What is meant by a 'composite' material? [2]
>
> *A material which contains two or more different materials that are combined[1] to create a material with improved properties and functionality[1].*

TECHNICAL TEXTILES

Technical textiles are manufactured for their function and performance.

They can be made from a combination of natural and synthetic fibres or filaments, and be coated, laminated or impregnated to improve the properties and performance of the finished item. Technical textiles are used in automotive and aerospace applications, for geotextiles and for agrotextiles.

Gore-Tex®

Gore-Tex is a fabric with breathable yet waterproof properties. It allows vapour produced by the wearer to escape, yet repels water making it an effective waterproof fabric commonly used for outdoor clothing.

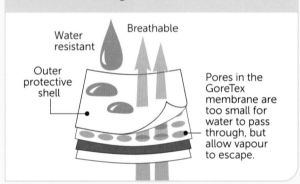

Water resistant

Breathable

Outer protective shell

Pores in the GoreTex membrane are too small for water to pass through, but allow vapour to escape.

Protective clothing

Protective clothing is used in sports, medical, hazardous and industrial environments and all incorporate technical textiles. They can provide:

- Chemical protection
- Particulate filtration
- Flame resistance
- Cut resistance
- Outdoor protection and high visibility

Kevlar®

Kevlar is a plastic fibre with high tensile strength. It is heat resistant and extremely hard-wearing. It is a flexible and lightweight synthetic fibre from the class of fibres known as aramids which are modified polyamide fibres. Polyamide molecules connect to form long chains. These are aligned parallel to each other inside the fibres acting as reinforcement to give Kevlar its strength. Kevlar fibres are so tightly spun, it's nearly impossible to separate them.

The tightly woven cloth is cut, puncture and ballistic resistant so is used to make body armour, bullet proof vests and many types of personal protective equipment. If a projectile hits Kevlar, the fibres 'catch' it, absorbing and dissipating its energy. It is also used to reinforce tyres, add strength and durability to sports equipment and many vehicle components.

1. Kevlar is used to produce body armour.

   Explain how Kevlar fibres are arranged to provide its protective properties.   [2]

   The fibres are tightly woven[1] to resist penetration.[1] The fibres absorb and dissipate an impact.[1]

Microfibres

Microfibres are synthetic fibres, less than one denier thick which can be micro-encapsulated. Micro-encapsulation is a process of adding a coating to tiny particles or droplets. The particles improve the properties of microfibre as they can hold anti-microbial agents, insecticides, moisturisers and medicines to be released under control.

Fire resistant fabrics

Fire resistant fabrics are designed to withstand heat and resist burning. They are primarily used for protective clothing for fire fighters. Heat and flame-resistant fibres such as Nomex® are woven to produce a fabric that provides protection against heat and flame without melting or dripping. As it is lightweight and durable, it is also used in racing driver and pit crew apparel. When Nomex is exposed to heat, its fibres thicken and absorb heat energy.

Conductive fabrics

Conductive fabrics are made from, coated or blended with, conductive metals. They can be used for thermal heating or allowing an electrical signal to pass through them with very little resistance. These e-textiles can also have batteries, small lights and electronics embedded into them, and are often fitted into sportswear to monitor vital statistics. Fibre based solar cells and kinetic energy harvesters are being woven into fabric to generate power from sunlight and motion.

2. Outdoor sports enthusiasts are able to purchase gloves that enable them to use a touch-screen phone whilst wearing the gloves.

   Explain how conductive fabrics can be used to deliver this functionality. [2]

   Thin, conductive metal fibres are woven into the glove fabric[1], which transfer the skin's natural charge through the glove to the fingertip[1] of the fabric and onto the screen[1].

SYSTEMS APPROACH TO DESIGNING

A system comprises parts or components that work together to control a task or activity.

Systems diagrams

Systems diagrams are often designed using a system block diagram that clearly lays out the **input**, **process** and **output** stages of a system.

Input	Process	Output
Switch	Heater on	Heat

In an electrical circuit, an input device receives an external signal, for instance from a switch. The process device receives the input information and determines the output. In the example above, the output is in the form of heat.

A process device processes information. It will take a signal from the input stage and act upon the instruction, for instance by counting or creating a time delay.

Inputs

Light dependent resistor (LDR)

Detects changes in light levels. Resistance increases in the dark and decreases in the light. Used in street lighting and security lights.

Pressure sensor

Detects changes in pressure in gases or liquids. Used to detect a leak in a fuel system triggering a warning light if the pressure falls.

Switch

Switches turn a circuit on or off. Types include push, slide or toggle. Used in lighting, control panels and power switches.

Temperature sensor

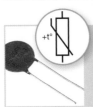

Detects a change in temperature. When the temperature increases, resistance decreases. Used in household appliances and vehicles.

Process

Resistor

Used to limit the flow of current and helps to protect some components from being overloaded.

Microcontroller

A programmable component is a chip, which is used in electrical products such as washing machines.

A car has a tyre pressure monitor that displays an alert on the dashboard if it detects a problem. State the input, process and output of this feature.

(a) Input.   (b) Process.   (c) Output.   [3]

(a) A pressure sensor detects a level of air pressure inside the tyre. [1]

(b) The pressure reading is compared to pre-set minimum and maximum levels. [1]

(c) A lamp / buzzer / speaker is used to alert the driver if the reading exceeds either the upper or lower limit. [1]

Processes

Components process electronic signals and enable output devices to perform tasks. These processes are controlled by small chips known as integrated circuits or ICs. A **microcontroller** is a tiny computer on a single chip with a processor core, memory and input and output (I/O) ports. They can perform the task of multiple ICs. They are designed to implement a specific function and are found in devices such as remote controls, appliances, toys and some power tools. They can be programmed in a variety of computer languages or software that uses flowcharts for programming.

Timers and counters

Microcontrollers can be programmed for decision making with counting and timing functions.

Timers are used for processes requiring a time-controlled output. A pulse of voltage at timed intervals will trigger an output. Counters store and can display the number of times an event or process has occurred.

Flowcharts

Flowcharts describe the operation of a program in simple terms.
A set of symbols are used to draw a flowchart.

Start and stop: show the start of a diagram and the exit point

Decision: used when there are 'Yes' an 'No' outcomes

Process: indicate the process that's happening

Arrow: indicates the flow of instructions

An **open loop system** may be represented by a flow chart that does not make decisions or loop back to a previous part of the diagram. A **closed loop system**, such as the one above, contains a decision and feedback arrow that leads back to a previous stage of the process.

START

Is belt secure? — Y

N

Buzzer on

Wait 0.5

Buzzer off

Wait 0.5

Outputs

Buzzer
Gives a sound output. Electromagnetic wires turn a circuit on and off to create a buzz. Used in doorbells and toys.

Lamp
Uses electricity to produce light of varying levels. Available in different sizes and power outputs. Used for household lighting.

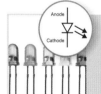

Light emitting diode (LED)
A low power light commonly used in power indicators and lamps. Long lasting.

Speaker
Speakers translate an electrical signal into an audible sound. Used in sound systems, laptops and radios.

MECHANICAL DEVICES

Mechanical devices can change one form of force to another. An input motion transforms into force to make an output motion.

Different types of movement

Linear motion is movement in one direction along a straight line.

Reciprocating motion. This is repetitive up-and-down or back-and-forth linear motion.

Rotary motion is movement on or around an axis.

Oscillating motion is movement backwards and forwards along a curved path.

Which type of motion best describes the movement of a sewing machine needle?   [1]

Reciprocating motion.[1]

Changing magnitude and direction of force

A lever is a very simple way to gain mechanical advantage (MA), making lifting or moving something much easier. It consists of a rigid bar that pivots or rotates about a fulcrum with a load applied.

A typical lever consists of:

Fulcrum - a pivot point around which a lever turns
Effort - an input force
Load - an output force

To calculate the mechanical advantage, use the following formula:

$$MA = \frac{Load}{Effort} = \frac{300N}{100N} = \frac{3}{1}$$ Also written as 3:1 or just MA of 3.

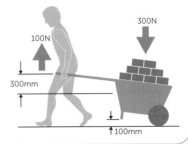

First order lever

First class levers have the fulcrum between the force and the load.

Example: Pliers.

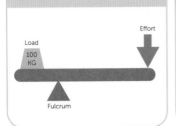

Second order lever

Second order levers (Class 2) are most easily remembered as having a wheelbarrow action. The fulcrum is at one end with the effort at the opposite end. The load is anywhere in the middle.

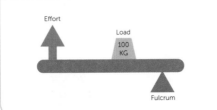

Third order lever

A Class 3 lever has the fulcrum at one end, the load at the opposite end and the effort applied in the middle.

Example: Tweezers.

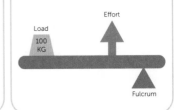

LINKAGES

A linkage is a mechanism made by connecting rigid parts. Linkages can change the magnitude of a force, change the direction of a force or transform it into a totally different motion.

Push pull

The push/pull linkage maintains the direction of the input motion so that the output travels in the same direction.

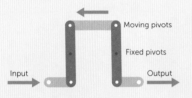

Bell crank

The bell crank linkage changes the direction of the input motion through 90°. It can be used to change horizontal motion into vertical motion or vice versa.

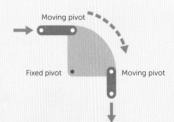

Rotary systems

Rotary systems are used to drive mechanisms in equipment and machinery. They transfer the direction of force along different paths and through changes of angle and direction.

A **cam** is mainly used to change rotary motion into reciprocating motion through the use of a **follower**. A crank is used to rotate the shaft, which rotates the cam and moves the follower up and down.

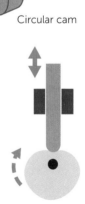

Circular cam or **eccentric cam** – steady rise and fall.

Pear cam – rapid rise and fall followed by long dwell (rest).

Snail cam – long dwell followed by steady rise and sudden drop. This can only turn in one direction, otherwise the mechanism would jam.

Heart shaped cam – slight rise and fall with no dwell period.

An child's toy crocodile has a mouth that slowly opens and snaps shut again when a handle is turned.

Suggest the most suitable cam to be used to create this mechanism. [1]

A snail cam.[1]

GEARS

Gears are toothed wheels, that mesh to transfer motion from one part of a machine to another. Gears are found in many things from cars and bicycles, to clocks and can openers.

A **gear train** transmits rotary motion and torque. **Torque** is a force that causes rotation. Different sized gears connect to increase or decrease the speed of rotation. They also increase or decrease the torque.

Gear train

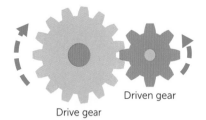

Drive gear
Driven gear

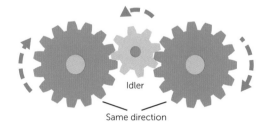

Idler
Same direction

Drive gear
The drive gear (input) turns the driven gear (output). The gears turn in opposite directions. The toothed wheels interlock to prevent slipping.

Idler gear
An idler gear is used to change the direction of rotation so that the driven gear turns in the same direction as the drive gear. It transfers movement from the drive gear to the driven, so size does not affect speed.

Calculating gear ratio

A gear ratio is the ratio between the drive gear and the driven gear. The relative sizes of two gear wheels determines how fast each will turn. A small gear with fewer teeth, will turn faster than a large gear with many teeth.

Count the number of teeth on each gear. Divide the number of teeth on the driven gear, by the number of teeth on the drive gear.

For example, if the drive gear has 40 teeth and the driven gear 20, the gear ratio is 20 divided by 40. 20/40 = 0.5 or expressed as a ratio is 1:2.

For every rotation of the drive gear, the driven gear rotates twice. This is referred to as gearing up.

Velocity ratio

To achieve maximum speed, have a larger driver gear paired with a smaller driven gear. The drive gear will be connected to the power source, for instance the pedals on a bicycle. Velocity ratios are calculated by dividing the drive gear by the driven gear.

A gear system of a simple toy train has a driver gear with 15 teeth attached to a motor and a driven gear with 30 teeth attached to the rear axle.

Calculate the gear ratio for the car. [1]

Driven / drive = 30 / 15 = 2:1 or 2. [1]

PULLEYS AND BELTS

Pulleys

Pulleys can help to lift a load providing a mechanical advantage. In machines, pulleys transmit rotary motion and force from the input or drive shaft to the output or driven shaft. For the movement to be transferred it's important the belt does not slip or stretch. Pulleys are not ideal for transmitting high torque due to their tendency to slip. Belts are often made of reinforced rubber or high strength materials such as Kevlar®.

Fixed pulley

A fixed pulley uses a wheel with a groove in it and a rope that sits in the groove. It allows you to change the direction of the force needed, which makes lifting easier, but the weight will feel the same.

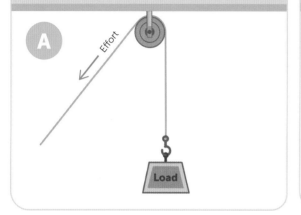

Block and tackle pulley

A block and tackle pulley uses two or more pulleys, one fixed and one moveable, to help reduce the amount of effort needed to lift a load. It provides a mechanical advantage making a load easier to lift.

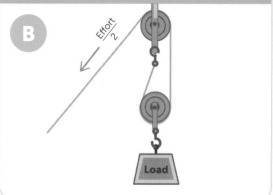

Look at the block and tackle pulley in diagram B above.

(a) Calculate the distance the rope will need to be pulled in order to raise the load by 1m. [1]

(b) Calculate the effort is required to raise a 120kg load. [1]

 (a) 1m height x 2 pulleys = 2m rope distance.[1] (b) 120kg / 2 pulleys = 60kg effort.[1]

Belts

A drive belt (loop of flexible rubber) connects two or more pulleys together. The belt transfers power from the pulley to the receiving system. In the instance of a car, a belt transfers engine power to the alternator to recharge the battery.

EXAMINATION PRACTICE

1. Explain the difference between renewable and non-renewable energy sources. [2]

2. Energy production fell in the UK from 2,619 TWh in 2004 to 1,465 TWh in 2016.
   (a) Calculate the percentage reduction in the amount of energy produced in the UK between 2004 and 2016. [2]
   (b) 21% of the UK's energy is supplied from nuclear sources.
       (i) Explain how energy is generated from nuclear power. [2]
       (ii) Give **one** similarity and **one** difference in the process of energy generation between using fossil fuels and nuclear fuels to generate power. [2]
       (iii) Explain why some people are against using nuclear energy. [2]

3. Explain **two** disadvantages of using biomass as an energy source. [4]

4. The photograph below shows a tidal barrage used to generate electricity.

   Explain **two** disadvantages of using a tidal barrage to generate electricity. [4]

5. Give **three** benefits of using rechargeable batteries rather than traditional alkaline batteries. [3]

6. A metals foam uses 25% of the mass of the base metal for its comparative size.
   (a) Calculate the mass of metal foam that is required to replace a solid 5.6 kg block of metal. [2]
   (b) Explain **one** reason why metal foams might be used to make aircraft parts. [2]

7. Give **two** ways in which nanomaterials have been used in the textiles industry. [2]

8. Explain what is meant by the term 'smart materials'. [2]

9. Which **one** of the following is a composite material? [1]
   (a) Titanium
   (b) Glassfibre Reinforced Plastic (GRP)
   (c) Polyester
   (d) Graphene

10. Titanium is usually alloyed with 6% aluminium and 4% vanadium.

    (a) Calculate the mass of vanadium required when making a 125kg batch of titanium alloy.   [2]

    (b) Explain **one** reason why pure titanium is used for artificial joints.   [2]

11. Describe **one** way in which micro-encapsulation is used in the textiles industry.   [2]

12. James has found the component below in his electronics kit.

    (a) Name the component shown.   [1]

    (b) Draw the circuit symbol for this component.   [1]

    (c) Give **two** applications for this component.   [2]

13. Draw a flowchart for the system given below.   [5]
- When the temperature is below 125, a heater is turned on.
- When the temperature is above 125, the heater is turned off.

14. The diagram below shows a push / pull linkage.

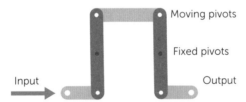

    Describe the action of the of the output if the input is moved 50mm to the right.   [2]

15. Give **two** disadvantages of using pulley and belts rather than a gear system to increase or decrease the velocity ratio.   [2]

16. The drawing below shows a simple gear train.

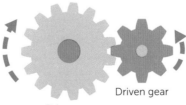

Driven gear

Drive gear

    Given the formula: gear ratio = teeth on driven gear / teeth on drive gear, calculate the gear ratio of the simple gear train if the driven gear has 8 teeth and the drive gear has 24 teeth.   [2]

PHYSICAL AND WORKING PROPERTIES

It is important to know the physical and working properties of a range of materials.

Physical properties

The physical properties of any material can be measured in their natural state.

Absorbency	The ability of a material to soak up or draw in heat, light or moisture.	Cotton is more absorbent than acrylic.
Density	The mass, per unit volume of any material. How solid is a material.	Polystyrene has a low density, suitable for packaging. Lead has high density, suitable for weights.
Electrical conductivity	The measure at which a material can transport electricity.	Copper is a good conductor of electricity. Insulators such as plastic or rubber do not conduct electricity.
Fusibility	The ability of a material to be converted from a solid to a fluid state by heat and combined with another material.	Good property for metals and polymers to aid casting and welding.
Thermal conductivity	The measure of a material's ability to transfer heat.	Copper is an excellent conductor of heat.

Working properties

Working properties describe how a material responds when it is manipulated or worked.

Ductility	The ability of a material to be stretched or drawn or pulled without breaking.	Copper is ductile so can be drawn out to make wire.	Describe the difference between toughness and hardness. [2]
Elasticity	The ability to return to its original shape after stretching or compression.	Lycra is used for sportswear to provide freedom of movement.	*Toughness is the ability of a material to withstand an energy or force before it becomes fractured.[1]*
Hardness	The ability to withstand impact, wear, abrasion and indentation.	Tungsten is hard, used for knives, drills and saws.	*Hardness is a measure of resistance to abrasion, wear, scratching, or penetration.[1]*
Malleability	The ability to be bent and shaped without cracking or splitting.	Gold, copper, silver and lead can all be easily hammered into shape.	
Strength	The ability to withstand a force such as pressure, compression, tension or shear.	May be strong in one force and not another. Concrete is strong under compression, but not tension.	
Toughness	The ability to absorb shock without fracturing.	Kevlar® body armour absorbs impact.	

PAPERS AND BOARDS

Paper

Paper is measured by weight in grams per square metre (**GSM**). Common weights range from 60–170gsm.

Layout

Properties: Medium opacity sheet with a smooth finish. 60–90 gsm.

Uses: Sketch and design work.

Tracing

Properties: Off white, low opacity sheet. 60-90 gsm.

Uses: Copying, overlays and tracing drawings.

Cartridge

Properties: Thick white paper with a textured surface. 120–150 gsm.

Uses: Sketching, watercolours, ink drawings.

Bleed proof

Properties: Thick, coated paper that prevents inks or marker pens from bleeding. 120–150 gsm.

Uses: High quality illustrations with colour richness and vibrancy.

Grid

Properties: White paper with a printed grid of squares, isometric lines or other patterns. 80–100 gsm.

Uses: Scale drawings, model making, scientific diagrams.

Card and board

Card weights range from 200gsm–350gsm. Board is selected by thickness and measured in **microns.**

Corrugated card

Properties: Two layers of lightweight card containing a fluted layer for strength.

Uses: Packaging for impact protection and insulation. Fully degradable and recyclable.

Foil-lined

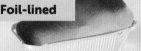

Properties: Card coated with aluminium foil on one side. Foil retains heat keeping contents warm and creates a moisture barrier.

Uses: Takeaway containers.

Duplex

Properties: Two layers of card bonded together, often with a white external layer. Available with metallic and holographic finishes.

Uses: Tough, with a bright white appearance suitable for packaging. Used with a waxy coating for food and drink containers.

Foam core

Properties: An inner foam core with a paper face. Rigid and stiff.

Uses: Model making and mounting artworks.

Ink jet

Properties: Treated card with smooth finish and bleed proof printable surface.

Uses: Printing photographs and artworks.

Solid white

Properties: High quality card, brilliant white smooth finish on both sides.

Uses: Greetings cards, quality packaging and book covers.

NATURAL TIMBERS

Hardwoods

Hardwood is from a **deciduous** tree, usually a broad-leafed variety that drops its leaves in the winter.

Ash

Properties: Flexible, tough and shock resistant, laminates well. Pale brown.

Uses: Sports equipment and tool handles.

Beech

Properties: Fine finish, tough and durable. Beige with pink hue.

Uses: Children's toys and models, furniture, veneers.

Mahogany

Properties: Easily worked, durable and finishes well. Reddish brown.

Uses: High end furniture and joinery, veneers.

Balsa

Properties: Very soft and spongy, good strength to weight ratio. Pale cream/white.

Uses: Prototyping and modelling.

Oak

Properties: Tough, hard and durable, high quality finish possible. Light brown.

Uses: Flooring, furniture, railway sleepers, veneers.

1. Give **two** differences between hardwood and softwood. [2]

   Hardwood comes from deciduous trees.[1]
   Softwood comes from coniferous trees.[1]
   Deciduous trees are usually slower growing which makes the wood denser.[1]

Softwoods

Softwood is from a **coniferous** tree, one that usually bears needles and has cones.

Pine

Properties: Lightweight, easy to work, can split and be resinous near knots. Pale yellowish brown.

Uses: Interior construction, furniture.

Spruce

Properties: Easy to work, high stiffness to weight ratio. Creamy white.

Uses: Construction, furniture and musical instruments.

Larch

Properties: Durable, tough, good water resistance, good surface finish. Pale reddish brown.

Uses: Exterior cladding, decking, flooring, machined mouldings, furniture and joinery. railway sleepers and veneers.

MANUFACTURED TIMBERS

Manufactured boards are usually sheets of processed natural timber waste products or veneers combined with adhesives. They are made from waste wood, low-grade timber and recycled timber.

Chipboard

Properties
Good compressive strength, not water resistant unless treated, good value but prone to chipping on edges and corners.

Uses
Flooring, low-end furniture, kitchen units and worktops.

Plywood

Properties
Very stable in all directions due to alternate layering at 90°, with outside layers running in the same direction.

Uses
Furniture, shelving, toys and construction. Interior, exterior and marine grades available for greater water resistance.

Medium density fibreboard (MDF)

Properties
Rigid and stable, with a smooth, easy to finish surface.
Very absorbent so not good in high humidity or damp areas.

Uses
Good value, flat pack furniture, toys, kitchen units and internal construction.

2. Arun is evaluating the use of natural timber over manufactured timber for a built-in wardrobe.

   (a) Give **two** advantages of using manufactured timber over natural timber. [2]

   (b) Give **two** disadvantages of using manufactured timber over natural timber. [2]

   (a) Manufactured board is available in large board sizes which can reduce the number of joins.[1] It is cheaper than natural timber[1], a good insulator[1], easily cut[1] and can be easily laminated to apply a wide range of finishes.[1]

   (b) Manufactured board is dense which makes it very heavy in large sheets.[1] Owing to the density and adhesive used in the production process, manufactured board can quickly blunt blades and cutting tools.[1] Resins and binders in manufactured board can be toxic so precautions must be taken.[1] Edges are difficult to finish due to no natural end grain.[1]

METALS

Ferrous metals

Ferrous metals all contain iron **ferrite** and have high tensile strength and durability.

- Most ferrous metals are magnetic.
- Vulnerable to rust if exposed to moisture without a protective finish.
- Stainless steel is protected from rust by the presence of chromium.

Low carbon / mild steel

Properties
Tough and ductile. Rusts easily if not protected.

Uses
Car bodies, steel building frames, pipelines.

High carbon steel

Properties
Hard, but brittle. Hard wearing, resists abrasion and retains its shape.

Uses
Tools, blades, scissors.

Cast iron

Properties
Hard but brittle. Resists deformation and rust.

Uses
Kitchen pans, machine bases, manhole covers.

Explain **two** factors that make metal an expensive material to obtain. [2]

Mining is dangerous and often very remote.[1] Mining machinery is very expensive to buy and operate[1] and techniques for extraction often use dynamite[1]. Significant electrical or heat energy is required to separate metal from its ore.[1]

Non-ferrous metals

Non-ferrous metals are a group of pure metals and do not contain iron.

- Non-magnetic so used for wiring and electronics.
- Non-ferrous metals have a higher resistance to rust but can corrode or oxidise.
- Commonly used externally for guttering, pipes and road signs.

Zinc

Properties: Brittle, yet malleable. High corrosion resistance.

Uses: Used to galvanise steel.

Copper

Properties: Ductile and malleable. Good electrical conductor.

Uses: Plumbing supplies, electrical cables.

Aluminium

Properties: Lightweight, ductile, resists corrosion.

Uses: Bike frames, drinks cans, takeaway trays.

Tin

Properties: Malleable and ductile, high corrosion resistance. Good electrical conductor.

Uses: Solder, plating surfaces such as cans.

ALLOYS

Alloys are a mixture of at least one pure metal and another element.

The alloying process combines the metals and other elements to improve working properties or aesthetics. Alloys are harder than pure metals as they contain atoms of different sizes. These distort the arrangement of the atoms making it hard for the layers of atoms to slide over each other, creating a harder, stronger metal.

High speed steel

Composition may include:
- Chromium Molybdenum
- Tungsten Vanadium
- Cobalt Carbon

Properties
Can withstand high temperatures when machining at high speed.

Uses
Cutting tools such as drill bits, mill cutters, taps and dies.

Stainless steel

Composition:
- Low carbon 0.03–0.08%
- Chromium 10.5–26%

Properties
Hard, ductile. Rust resistant. Chromium layer protects steel from corrosion.

Uses
Cutlery, kitchen and medical equipment.

Brass

Composition:
- Copper: 65%
- Zinc: 35%

Properties
Malleable and easily cast. Good corrosion resistance.

Uses
Musical instruments, plumbing fitments and ornate artefacts.

Explain **one** advantage of alloys over pure metals.   [2]

An alloy can take on the properties of each of its component metals[1] making it more suitable for specific tasks.[1] Alloys are generally harder than pure metals[1] since they are made of different sized molecules which makes the layers more difficult to slide over each other[1]. An alloy often has better corrosion resistance than a pure metal[1] and can be more easily manipulated into different forms[1].

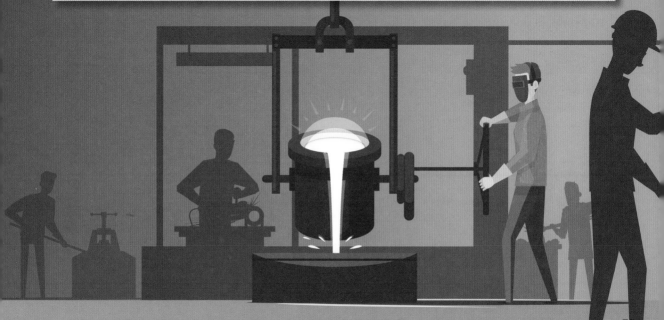

THERMOFORMING POLYMERS

Plastics are mainly synthetic materials made from **polymers** traditionally derived from finite petrochemical resources. Naturally occurring plastics include amber and rubber.

Thermoforming polymers are generally more flexible than thermosets, especially when heated. This is owing to their physical structure; polymer chains are quite loosely entangled with very few cross links. This allows the chains to easily slide past each other when heated. They can be formed into complex shapes and reformed multiple times.

Polypropylene (PP)

Properties
Flexible, tough, lightweight, food safe.

Uses
Kitchen, medical products, rope.

High density polyethylene (HDPE)

Properties
Lightweight, rip and chemical resistant.

Uses
Milk bottles, pipes, crates, wheelie bins.

High impact polystyrene (HIPS)

Properties
Flexible, impact resistant, lightweight, can be food safe, used for vacuum forming.

Uses
Yoghurt pots, vacuum formed products.

Polyethylene terephthalate (PET)

Properties
Blow moulded, chemically resistant and fully recyclable.

Uses
Drinks bottles, food containers, yarn.

Acrylic (PMMA)

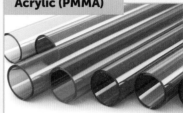

Properties
Tough but brittle when thin. Easily scratched, formed and bonded.

Uses
Car lights, alternative to glass, modern baths, clothing.

Polyvinyl chloride (PVC)

Properties
Flexible, easily extruded, tough and resistant to chemicals.

Uses
Raincoats, pipes, electrical tape.

THERMOSETTING POLYMERS

Thermosetting polymers undergo a chemical change and once formed or set, cannot be reformed. Thermosets are resistant to higher temperatures but tend to burn when heated rather than melt. They are harder, more brittle and provide good insulation and chemical resistance.

Polyester resin (PR)

Properties
Good electrical insulator, hard, but becomes tough when mixed with glass strands to form glass reinforced plastic (GRP).

Uses
Encapsulation, boat hulls as GRP.

Urea formaldehyde (UF)

Properties
High tensile strength, heat resistant, good electrical insulator, hard, brittle, easily injection moulded.

Uses
Adhesives for bonding particle boards, decorative laminates, electrical casings.

Epoxy resin (ER)

Properties
Good strength to weight ratio, good electrical insulator, heat resistant.

Uses
Bonding waterproof coatings, electronic circuit boards.

Phenol formaldehyde (PF)

Properties
Heat resistant and a good electrical insulator.

Uses
Heat resistant handles, electrical components, snooker balls.

Melamine formaldehyde (MF)

Properties
Lightweight, hard but brittle.

Uses
Worktops, surfaces, some kitchenware.

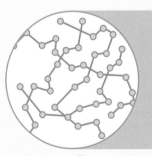

Thermoforming plastics are more flexible and have loose polymer chains that break apart when heated.

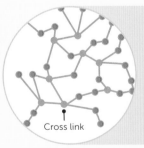

Cross link

Thermosetting plastics have rigid cross-linked polymer chains that set when heated and cannot be reformed.

Explain why thermosetting polymers are more difficult to recycle than thermoforming polymers. [2]

The molecular structure of thermosets is more rigid,[1] making them difficult to reform once 'set'[1]. When thermosets are reheated,[1] they often tend to burn rather than melt[1].

TEXTILES

Textiles are derived from natural and synthetic materials. They are highly adaptable and can be constructed to maximise their different properties.

Natural fibres

Natural fibres are made from plant- or animal-based fibres and are renewable.

Cotton

Sourced from cotton plant.

Properties
Soft, strong, absorbent. Washes and takes dyes well.

Uses
Range of clothing, towels, bed sheets.

Silk

Sourced from silkworm cocoon.

Properties
Soft, fine, lightweight. Natural shine due to its triangular structure.

Uses
Luxury clothing, underwear, ties, wall hangings, night clothes.

Wool

Sourced from sheep, goats, rabbits, camelids.

Properties
Warm, naturally crease resistant, can shrink.

Uses
Jumpers, coats, suits, blankets, carpets.

Synthetic fibres

Synthetic fibres are made from chemically produced polymers.

Polyamide (Nylon)

Properties
Strong and hard wearing, resists creasing.

Uses
Rope, webbing, parachutes, sportswear, umbrellas.

Elastane (Lycra)

Properties
Smooth, strong and elastic or stretchy. Retains its shape and quick drying.

Uses
Sportswear, swimwear, surgical supports.

Polyester

Properties
Tough, strong, hard wearing, non-absorbent.

Uses
Fleece, backpacks, threads, sportswear.

Blended fibres

Blended and mixed fibres combine two or more types of fibre to produce a fabric with useful properties.

Polycotton

Properties
Durable and stronger than pure cotton. Reduces creasing.

Uses
Clothing and bed sheets.

Give the source or raw materials used to make each of the following textiles:

(a) Polyester   (b) Wool
(c) Cotton   [3]

*(a) Oil.[1] (b) Animal fleece.[1]
(c) Cotton plant.[1]*

WOVEN AND NON-WOVEN TEXTILES

Woven cloth

Woven cloth is made up of two sets of yarns which are threaded at 90 degrees to each other. The **warp** threads are fixed in the loom and run the length of the fabric. The **weft** threads run across the width of the fabric.

Plain weave

Properties: Strong, hard-wearing, retains shape. Even surface on both sides. Different yarns can create hard wearing weave.

Uses: Tablecloths, upholstery, clothing.

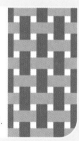

Non-woven fabric

Non-woven fabrics are made directly from fibres without being spun into yarns.

Bonded fabric

Properties: Fabrics lack strength, they have no grain so can be cut in any direction and do not fray.

Uses: Disposable hygienic clothing, cloths, teabags.

Felted fabric

Properties: Can be formed with moisture and heat; once dry it has no elasticity and can be pulled apart.

Uses: Hats, handicrafts, protective pads.

Knitted fabric

Knitting is a technique of interlocking yarn loops together to produce a fabric. Used for jumpers, socks, tights, and soft toys.

A child's T-shirt is made using a plain weave fabric. Give **two** features of this type of material. [2]

Plain weave fabrics have an even surface and appear the same on both sides.[1] It is suitable for printing on.[1] It's a smooth, even fabric which maintains shape.[1] The spacing in the yarn will determine how thick or soft the fabric is.[1]

Weft knitting

Weft knit fabrics are made by hand or by machine using a single yarn that forms interlocking loops across the width of the fabric. Stretchy and can lose its shape.

Warp knitting

Warp knitting is made by machine which forms interlocking vertical loops. Less stretchy so holds it shape better.

EXAMINATION PRACTICE

1. Paper is measured in GSM. State what is meant by GSM.   [1]

2. State which type of paper is shown in the image below.   [1]

3. Give the specific type of paper described below.   [1]

   An off white, low opacity sheet. Its transparency decreases as GSM increases.

4. Give **two** properties of corrugated cardboard that make it an appropriate choice of material for a takeaway pizza box.   [2]

5. Which **one** of the following is a manufactured timber?   [1]

   (a) Oak   (b) Chipboard   (c) Pine   (d) Ash

6. Give **two** properties of ash that make it an appropriate choice of material for a hockey stick.   [2]

7. Explain **one** reason why oak is an appropriate choice of material for wooden floorboards.   [2]

8. Mild steel is a ferrous metal and stainless steel is an alloy.

   (a) Name the **two** key elements alloyed to make stainless steel.   [2]

   (b) Give **two** applications of mild steel.   [2]

9. Which metal is reddish brown in colour and oxidises with a green/grey appearance?   [1]

10. Give **two** properties of urea formaldehyde that make it an appropriate choice of material for an electrical light switch.   [2]

11. Explain **one** reason why high impact polystyrene (HIPS) is an appropriate choice of materials to make yoghurt pots.   [2]

12. Explain **one** reason why copper electrical cables are coated in PVC.   [2]

13. Which **one** of the following is a natural fibre?   [1]

    (a) Lycra   (b) Polyester   (c) Nylon   (d) Cotton

14. Give **two** properties of silk.   [2]

15. Give **two** applications of polyester for textiles-based products.   [2]

16. Explain what is meant by the term elasticity.   [2]

SECTION B
3.2 SPECIALIST TECHNICAL PRINCIPLES

Information

At least 15% of the exam will assess maths and at least 10% will assess science.

All dimensions are in millimetres.

The marks for questions are shown in brackets.

The maximum mark for this paper is 100.

There are 20 marks for Section A, 30 marks for Section B and 50 marks for Section C.

Specification areas 3.2.1 to 3.2.9 are covered in this Section. Some content has been covered in other sections where it relates more closely to the materials or techniques covered elsewhere.

SELECTION OF MATERIALS OR COMPONENTS

There are many factors to consider when choosing the right materials for the design of a product.

Aesthetics

In product design, designers consider aesthetic factors including shape, size, colour, surface finish and texture. Aesthetics should appeal to the target market.

Functionality

Designers must ensure that the chosen material is fit for purpose. They need to understand the purpose of the end product; will the material do the job it's selected for and will it be easy to work with?

Availability

Designers must consider the availability of a material. Issues with supply can affect the price of the end-product.

- Are the materials easy to source?
- Are they widely available and quick to deliver?
- Are they supplied in stock forms and sizes?

Social factors

Designers have a social responsibility to consider what impact their products may have on the environment. Factors for consideration include:

- Using materials from sustainable sources.
- Sourcing materials that have a positive impact on farmers and workers.
- Reducing the use of unethically sourced materials that harm the environment.
- Using recycled products.

Cultural factors

Designers should consider the ideas and customs of different cultures in our society. Gender, religion and wealth all affect our lifestyle and choices. The views of one culture may vary from another. This can be as simple as the choice of colour, or how a product is named or advertised.

Cost

The cost of materials will impact the final price a product can be sold for. The overall cost of design, materials, manufacture, testing, packaging and delivery should not exceed the selling price.

Mass produced, budget items will need to be made of cheaper and readily available materials. High-end luxury items will need to be made of high-quality materials to reflect the selling price.

Buying materials and components in bulk reduces the cost per unit, helping to reduce the overall cost of manufacturing. The disadvantages to this are the upfront costs, extra storage space needed and potential wastage of any goods with a shelf life that expires.

Ethical factors

Design should consider the needs of the user; understand the requirements they have and make their product solve these problems. As part of this process designers should:

- Consider human rights.
- Make something functional, reliable and usable.
- Consider the users experience and make life better.

Manufacturers should avoid using unethical materials that exploit the workforce or damage the environment during their production. Wood or paper products that carry the Forest Stewardship Council® (FSC) logo, show that they come from a sustainable source. The FSC certifies materials that are sourced from sustainably managed forests. This means the forest will use selective logging and replanting to create a cycle of productivity and supply that doesn't harm the forest environment.

Environmental factors

When selecting materials, designers should aim to limit the environmental impact of their product.

- Is it possible to use a sustainable material?
- Can the materials be sourced locally?
- How easy is it to extract and transport the materials?
- Can they be reused, recycled or are they biodegradable?

Consider one of the following materials used in the manufacture of different products.

Tropical hardwood   Fur   Aluminium   Urea formaldehyde   Cotton

Discuss the ethical, social and environmental factors that should be considered for your chosen material. [4]

Tropical hardwood must be sourced from a sustainable FSC registered plantation.[1] Sustainable management protects tropical forests from illegal logging[1] which is increasing deforestation[1]. Illegal supply can continue to create demand for these timbers[1].

Fur was traditionally worn for warmth and protection. Now it is considered an unacceptable choice and a cruel practice[1]. Fur requires complex processing and treatments to make it suitable for clothing.[1] The chemicals and bi-products are detrimental to both the workforce and the environment[1] and need careful waste disposal[1].

Aluminium is a metal used in electronics casings and other metal items. Whilst it is plentiful, the extraction using electrolysis is very energy hungry.[1] Extracting and transporting aluminium from mines is dangerous[1], polluting[1] and scars the local environment[1]. Reuse and recycling are essential to reduce the consumption of energy[1].

Urea formaldehyde requires the extraction of oil[1] to manufacture into a polymer. It is a thermosetting polymer which means it is very difficult to recycle.[1] This increases landfill[1] and is becoming increasingly unpopular with individuals and pressure groups from an environmental perspective[1].

Cotton is grown extensively and provides employment in many developing countries[1]. It uses significant amounts of water and insecticides to grow the plants.[1] This is causing pollution[1] and water scarcity[1] in some countries. Organic cotton avoids the use of synthetic chemicals.[1] Sustainable production introduces improved irrigation and ecological growing methods[1] to minimise the harmful impact of conventional growing practises[1].

FORCES AND STRESSES

Materials and objects

All materials, structures and products must withstand stress as certain forces are applied to them when in use. The ability to withstand stress is what allows them to perform their functions successfully.

Bending

Bending is both tension and compression forces; tension on one side with compression on the other.

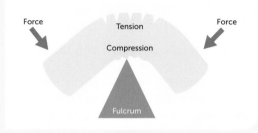

Compression

Compression occurs when a pushing force is applied to either end of a material

Explain **one** force acting on a pair of pliers when gripping a nail head. [2]

The handles will be subject to a bending force.[1] The outer edge of the handles will be under tension[1], whilst the insides will be under slight compression[1]. There will be a shear force acting on the pivot or fulcrum as the pliers are squeezed around the nail head.[1]

Torsion

Torsion forces occur when a material is twisted.

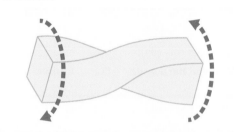

Tension

Tension occurs when a pulling force is applied to either end of a material.

Shear

Shear force acts on an object in a direction perpendicular to its length

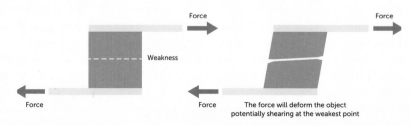

The force will deform the object potentially shearing at the weakest point

ENHANCING MATERIALS

Materials can be enhanced to resist or work with a variety of forces and stresses. This can improve functionality. They may be:

- **Reinforced** – strengthened by the addition of other materials.
- **Strengthened** – made stronger or more rigid to resist certain forces.
- Made more **flexible**.

Bending

Adding curves, arches and tubes can add considerable strength to products, using a minimum amount of material.

Folding

This can add strength, but also flexibility by enabling a material to bend easily.

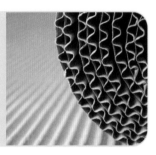

Fabric interfacing

Used in textiles, this adds an additional layer to give structure, shape and support.

Lamination

By bonding two or more materials together, a product's strength and stability are improved. It can also add to the aesthetics by giving a new finish.

Webbing

A strong fabric made from high-strength material, it is usually woven into flat strips and used for items under high tension.

Give **one** example of how lamination is used with a material of your choice. [2]

Answers may include: Lamination of manufactured timbers with melamine or polymer laminate.[1] Natural wood veneers used to laminate cheaper timber.[1] Laminated plywood in layers each at 90 degrees[1] to each other. Lamination of fabrics to improve strength and rigidity.[1] Lamination of different materials, for example, polymer and glass in windscreens[1], or polymer and paper laminate to provide protection from moisture and to add stiffness[1].

ECOLOGICAL AND SOCIAL FOOTPRINT

Product miles

This is the number of miles a product travels from all stages of manufacture through to its final retail destination. For example, a bicycle may be made up of frame components from China, gearing and mechanisms from the USA, tyres from Germany, and an English handmade saddle.

The finished product is then distributed to a wholesaler or shop anywhere in the world. Once sold, it travels once again to the consumer. At the end of its useful life the bicycle should be recycled. The recycled components may travel again to an appropriate recycling plant.

By adding up the mileage for each section of the product's journey, the total product mileage can be calculated. Using a carbon footprint calculator, the total CO_2 emissions can be calculated. This calculation is part of the **life cycle assessment**. Further detail on the LCA is covered in section 3.1.1.

Carbon emissions

In manufacturing goods, we consume energy which emits greenhouse gases. In order to reduce carbon emissions our production and consumption of energy needs to be reduced. Becoming more energy efficient, using low or no-carbon fuels and using new technologies such as carbon capture and storage all help.

Mining

Mining extracts minerals, metals and coal from the earth. The environment is adversely affected by soil erosion, air and water pollution and a loss of biodiversity. Mining creates open pits in the landscape, piles of waste and a potential risk of sinkholes. Mining companies are expected to return the land back to its original state after extraction.

Social factors

Designers have a social responsibility to consider what impact their products may have on the environment. Factors for consideration include:

- Using materials from sustainable sources.
- Sourcing materials that have a positive impact on farmers and workers.
- Reducing the use of unethically sourced materials that harm the environment.
- Using recycled products.

Deforestation

Deforestation is the permanent removal of trees to use the land for alternative means, such as agriculture. This results in a loss of wild habitat. Trees remove CO_2 from the atmosphere so when large areas are cut down, this contributes to an increase in CO_2 levels. Timber sourced from a sustainably managed forest means new trees are replanted to replenish supply.

Farming

Farming and agriculture rears animals and crops for food production. Although essential for sustaining human life, some farming practises have an impact on the environment. Pesticides and fertilisers, used to improve yield, can result in pollutants in water run-off from the soil, harming habitats and wildlife.

THE SIX Rs

Both designers and consumers should consider the six Rs in order to reduce the impact on the environment and improve sustainability.

1	**Rethink**	Consider the design and its impact. Is there a better way to produce it?
2	**Refuse**	Avoid using materials that are environmentally or socially unacceptable. Don't buy a product if you don't need it.
3	**Reduce**	Make products that are durable and long-lasting, reducing consumption and waste. Reduce energy and transport.
4	**Reuse**	The product may be used again by another person or reused for another purpose.
5	**Repair**	Repair where possible rather than replace.
6	**Recycle**	Take the product apart and convert parts into usable materials once again.

Explain why the six Rs are placed in the order that they appear above. [2]

There is an order of precedence. It is better to rethink and refuse to use a product at all as it saves having to consider any of the points thereafter.[1] Repair involves new parts that reuse does not.[1] Recycling is the last chance to retrieve some value from the materials used in an existing product.[1]

SAFE WORKING CONDITIONS

The Health and Safety at Work Act 1974 provides companies and employers with rules on how to protect people from injury or illness at their place of work.

- Workers should be provided with safe working conditions, given training and appropriate safety equipment for their environment.

- Laws are also in place to ensure safe working hours, appropriate wages and working conditions.

- Not all countries provide the same protection. Low paid workers may be exploited.

SOCIAL ISSUES IN THE DESIGN AND MANUFACTURE OF PRODUCTS

Reducing atmospheric pollution

Particles and gases that are suspended in the air cause atmospheric pollution. These can come from burning fossil fuels such as vehicle exhaust fumes and factory fumes. Wildfires also contribute to air pollution. These can all be serious to human health. Reductions can be made by:

- Switching from diesel and petrol to electric vehicles.
- Reducing the number of journeys made.
- Improving the recycling of materials used to produce cars and trucks.
- Increased use of alternative forms of energy such as solar, wind and tidal.
- Using energy efficient lighting and appliances.

Social footprint of a product

Increasingly, consumers look for products that are sustainable and responsible. Companies are considering all aspects of production from cradle to grave including:

- The complete supply chain involving workers, farmers and methods of transport.
- Developing new and innovative products that reduce the impact on the environment and resources.
- Being environmentally responsible and reducing the use and release of chemicals and toxins.

Reducing oceanic pollution

Our oceans are being filled with two types of pollution; chemicals and marine debris. Chemical pollution can be caused by run-off of agricultural fertilisers into waterways, oil spills, sewage or industrial chemical waste being released into the oceans. Plastic makes up approximately 75% of marine litter.

We can help reduce pollution by:

- Using plastic free alternatives and saying no to single use plastics such as straws, cups and plastic bags.
- Urge producers to make plastic free containers and packaging. Utilise biodegradable materials, eliminate micro-beads.
- Reduce our **carbon footprint** as increased greenhouse gases are making the oceans more acidic.
- Significantly increase recycling to reduce waste being dumped in the oceans.

EXAMINATION PRACTICE

1. Give **three** environmental factors designers should consider when selecting materials
   for a product. [3]

2. Explain what is meant by the logo shown below. [1]

3. State which type of force would be acting on each leg of a four-legged chair when it is sat on. [1]

4. The paper fan shown below has been manipulated to improve its function.
   State and describe **one** enhancement that helps it resist and work with different forces. [3]

5. Explain what is meant by the term 'lamination' when used as a technique to enhance a
   material's property. [2]

6. Aluminium cans are manufactured and distributed worldwide.

   (a) Explain what is meant by the term 'product miles'. [2]
   (b) Evaluate how product miles are likely to accumulate at each stage in the lifecycle of
       an aluminium can. [4]

7. State **two** ways in which a company could reduce its carbon emissions. [2]

8. Explain why recycling is often considered to be the last of the 6 Rs. [2]

9. Give **two** ways in which oceanic pollution can be reduced. [2]

10. Which of these is **not** a method for strengthening and enhancing a material? [1]
    (a) Webbing   (b) Laminating   (c) Drilling   (d) Interfacing

SOURCES AND ORIGINS

Paper and board are made from pulp. Pulp is a mixture of water and cellulose fibres, that are sourced from wood or certain plant fibres such as flax, hemp or bamboo. Softwoods are commonly used to create wood pulp as the fibres are longer, making a stronger paper.

Paper making process

Source material
Trees or grasses are cut and taken to a paper mill. Timber is debarked and chipped

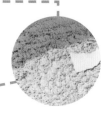

Pulp
Chips are added to a chemical solution and cooked to separate the cellulose fibres and produce a pulp.

Pulp
The pulp is pounded and squeezed. Chemicals, chalks or clays are added which alter the opacity of the final paper product.

Pulp
The end liquid is then bleached or dyed to the desired colour.

Sizing
Liquid pulp is mixed with additives to produce different types of paper finish. The sizing process affects the absorbency of the paper. Paper with little sizing is very absorbent.

Pulp to paper
Pulp is fed onto a mesh conveyor, and then passed through a series of rollers to remove excess water.

Calendering
After a series of drying rollers, the paper passes through calender rollers which give the paper its final finish.

1. Explain why softwoods are more environmentally friendly for making paper pulp. [2]

Softwood trees grow more quickly[1] and absorb more CO_2 during their growth period.[1] The output of paper pulp per hectare of planted forest is higher over time.[1] Softwood also has fewer impurities which require less processing to remove.[1]

Paper life cycle assessment

A **life cycle assessment (LCA)** considers the whole life cycle of a product 'from cradle to grave' i.e. from raw material extraction through to end of life. An LCA enables a manufacturer to calculate the quantities of raw material, energy and waste materials used and their impact on the environment.

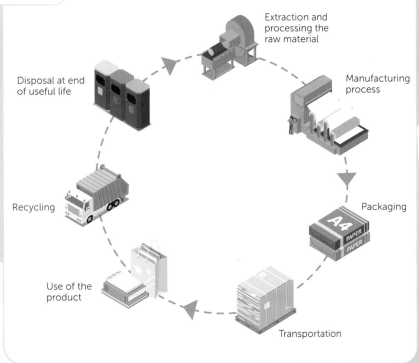

Extraction and processing the raw material

Manufacturing process

Disposal at end of useful life

Packaging

Recycling

Use of the product

Transportation

Recycled paper and board

Recycling is an important stage in the paper cycle. The amount of paper that is recycled continues to increase, which benefits manufacturing and the environment. Used paper and board is collected, graded and cleaned to remove inks and contaminants. Wood-pulp fibres can be recycled several times, but eventually they lose their paper making qualities when they become too short.

New wood pulp is continually needed for the papermaking process. Many paper companies now work with responsible forest management to ensure trees are planted to replace those that have been cut down.

Each time paper is recycled, environmental savings are made. If paper is sent to landfill it decomposes producing a greenhouse gas called methane. If recycled, less energy is used to make paper from wastepaper, which reduces the CO_2 emissions. Recycling paper and boards reduces the number of trees cut down.

2. Give **two** effects that the paper production process has on the environment. [2]

3. State the purpose of a life cycle assessment. [1]

2. Trees are felled to produce wood pulp for paper manufacture.[1] Trees provide a natural wildlife habitat[1] and absorb carbon dioxide[1]. The manufacturing process uses energy[1] and produces waste material that requires responsible disposal[1]. Production can create a monoculture.[1]

3. A life cycle assessment informs you of the carbon footprint[1] or the impact that the manufacture of a product has on the environment.[1]

PROPERTIES

The physical and mechanical properties of different paper and board affect their use in commercial applications.

Flyers and leaflets

Flyers are single sheet, printed material on a lightweight low-grade paper stock. A bleed proof, gloss paper will produce a clear form of printed matter suitable for promotional material, that will have a short life-span.

Leaflets are often folded or tri-folded. they are typically a higher quality print product containing more information that may be kept.

Both can be produced on biodegradable and recyclable paper.

Packaging that has a treatment or coating such as plastic, aluminium or wax is harder to recycle. Due to the cost of separating the materials, it often ends up in landfill.

Packaging for food

Cardboard needs a combination of properties to make it suitable for food-based packaging. It may need to be non-toxic, strong, waterproof, suitable for printing on, or airtight.

Card will need to be treated to improve functionality and be waterproof or greaseproof. It will need to be coated with plastics or aluminium to prevent leakage, entry of light and air, or to retain heat.

Corrugated card gives added rigidity and helps retain heat so is often used for takeaway pizza boxes. The boxes remain lightweight and can be stacked.

Modification of properties for specific purposes

The properties of paper and board can be enhanced for a specific use. During manufacture at the sizing stage, additives can be added to improve absorbency, brightness or reduce moisture transfer.

Paper towel
Can be treated with resins to retain the towel's structure when wet to prevent tearing and increase absorbency.

White board
Stiff board with a wax coating or laminated with polyethylene makes it suitable as a container for take-away food.

Baking parchment
The pulp is passed through a bath of sulfuric acid to gelatinise the surface and make it non-stick.

STOCK FORMS, TYPES AND SIZES

Stock form is the form in which a product can be bought and stored ready for use. Paper can be supplied in ply, rolls and sheets.

Ply	**Rolls**	**Sheets**

Ply contains layered sheets often in rolls.	Rolls for continuous run are used by the print industry for high volume printing such as books or newspapers.	Sheet form is used for office and domestic use, digital printing and art supplies. It can be in a variety of colours.

Weight and thickness

Paper is measured in **grams per square metre** (**gsm**). The lightest tissue paper ranges from 10–35 gsm. Most A4 copy paper is 80 gsm. Material up to and including 200 gms is paper, and over 200 gsm is classed as board.

Board is measured by thickness rather than weight and is measured in microns. 1 micron (1µm) is 1/1000th of a millimetre.

Corrugated card is produced in sheets from A4–A0, rolls and tubes and in flat-pack packaging. It is produced with either a single wall or a double wall for increased rigidity and stiffness.

Cartridge paper is commonly supplied in pads from A5–A2. Paper with a weight of 120 gsm is suitable for pencil and charcoal sketching. A heavier weight of 200 gsm is suited to watercolour and acrylic painting.

> Collect samples of different types of papers and boards. Compare factors such as sizing, weight, colour density, absorption and flexibility. Record your findings in a grid and compare with a friend.

Paper sizes

International Standards Organisation (**ISO**) set paper sizes. The A series of paper is defined by the ISO 216 standard. It is based on each size being half the size of the previous one, when folded parallel to the shorter length.

Copy paper is commonly used in offices and schools at A4 and A3 size, with a weight of between 80-100 gsm.

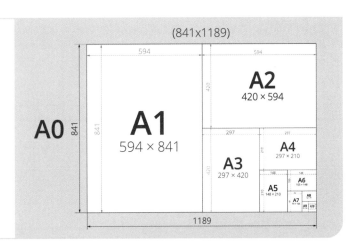

STANDARD COMPONENTS

Paper fasteners, seals and bindings

These are commonly used components that a manufacturer would purchase rather than making themselves. Use of standard components increases efficiency and can be purchased in bulk to keep costs down. Designers should factor in the use of standard components when working on a new product.

Bindings

Binding methods are used to hold together larger quantities of paper such as a brochure, book or presentation document.

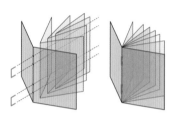
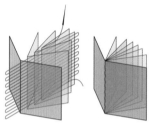

Saddle stitch binding
Used for thin books or notebooks. Thread or staples bind the paper together. It's a fast and cheap method for mass production.

Section sewn binding
Printed, folded sheets are sewn together to produce a high-quality and secure form of binding. Commonly used in hard back books.

Perfect binding
Used for softcover books. Pages are folded and glued into the cover sheet to form a spine.

Comb / spiral binding
A binding machine punches multiple holes into the side of a stack of paper. The comb or spiral is fed through the holes to hold the document together and enable the pages to be turned.

Slide binder
Durable, plastic spine bars which slide over the edges of a stack of paper to hold it together.

Fasteners

Fasteners are temporary ways of attaching paper and card together.

Paper fastener / split pin
The fastener is placed into a punched hole in sheets of paper. The brass legs are separated and bent over to secure the paper together

Binder clip
Metal clip that holds sheets of paper together, keeping them intact. The handles can be folded flat for stacking or upright for hanging documents.

Staple
A durable metal fastener used with a stapler to attach sheets of paper together. Heavy duty staples are available to secure cardboard packaging.

Paper clip
Steel wire is bent into a loop to create two tongues, which hold sheets of paper between them.

Treasury tag
A short cross piece of metal or plastic is passed through a hole in multiple sheets of paper. The strings are available in a variety of lengths.

Seals

Seals are used to bond paper or card. They make envelopes or packages secure or tamper-proof. This lets the recipient know that an item has been delivered unopened and intact.

Tamper-proof sticker
Labels that self-destruct when they are peeled. Useful for valuable packages.

Peel and seal envelope
Peel off the strip to reveal the adhesive and seal the envelope shut.

Wax seal
A dot of melted wax is used to seal paper. A pattern or crest can be pressed into the wax as a form of identity. The wax hardens quickly forming a hard bond.

Gummed envelope
A strip of water-soluble glue is on the edge of the flap. The glue is activated by licking or moistening, and the flap pressed to close.

COMMERCIAL PROCESSES, SURFACE TREATMENTS AND FINISHES

Different finishes can be applied to papers and boards to enhance appearance and improve function.

Printing

Printing is used on both papers and boards to improve visual appearance.

Screen printing

This is an effective technique for creating bold and striking prints for posters and artwork, and for printing on fabrics, particularly t-shirt design.

- A frame is covered with a tight, fine mesh – this is the screen.
- The chosen design or text is set into the mesh with a layer of light-reactive emulsion which hardens under bright light, producing the desired stencil.
- Printing ink is poured over the screen and pressed through the fine mesh to create a printed design on the paper or fabric below.
- The stencil can be used multiple times so is efficient for producing batches of identical designs.

Flexography

'Flexo' printing accommodates a wide variety of materials that don't have to be flat. Examples include plastics, cellophane, metallic film and plastics. These can be used in flexible packaging, gift wrap, textiles, carrier bags and wallpaper.

It is a high-speed process made for large print orders. It uses rolls of substrate to print high quantities without interruption. Flexography uses the 4-colour process **CMYK**.

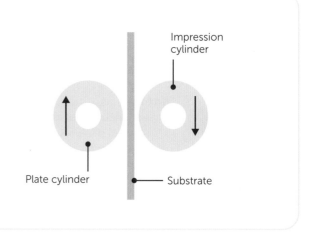

Gravure

Gravure printing produces excellent print quality, particularly fine detail and is used for very high print volumes such as postage stamps, catalogues, greetings cards and high-volume print advertising.

Gravure acid-etches an image on the surface of the metal printing surface. The etched areas are known as cells. The cells hold the ink that is transferred to the printable surface.

Embossing

Paper embossing creates a raised design on the paper surface, whereas debossing creates a recessed pattern.

Paper or card is placed between two dies, one raised and one recessed. The dies fit each other so when the paper is pressed between them, a permanent impression is made.

Embossing is used to add a high-quality finish to luxury card and paper products. It is also used for Braille labelling on medicines for the visually impaired.

Offset lithography

Also called **offset printing**, this is an indirect printing process. The inked image is transferred from the printing surface to a rubber blanket and then onto a flat printing surface, such as paper or board. Ink rollers transfer the ink on to the image areas and water rollers apply a water-based film to the non-image areas.

The **CMYK** colour model is used in colour printing. This refers to the four ink plates used: **cyan**, **magenta**, **yellow** and **key**, which is black. The print process is repeated for each colour.

This colour process is used for high volume print runs such as books, magazines and newspapers.

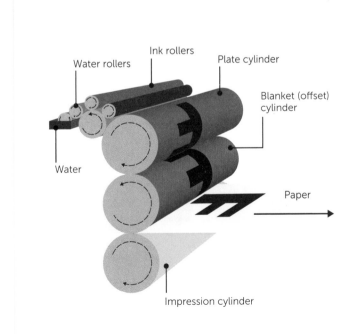

Water rollers
Ink rollers
Plate cylinder
Blanket (offset) cylinder
Water
Paper
Impression cylinder

Digital printing

Digital printing includes inkjet and laser printers. It is used for low volume, professional print runs and home/office printing.

It also uses the CMYK four colour process, but it is not necessary to create printing plates. The computer provides the printing instruction for the printer to add the correct layers of cyan, magenta, yellow and black ink to print the document.

Finishes

Varnishing

Varnishing applies a coating to a printed surface. It is a clear coating and usually used to prevent rubbing or scuffing for instance on magazines, postcards or printed material that has frequent handling. It is also used on playing cards to enable them to slide easily.

UV Varnishing

This can be a gloss or matt coating or used as a spot varnish to pick out a feature, such as a logo on a business card or the title on a book cover. It is dried instantly under UV light rather than with heat, so no solvents enter the atmosphere.

Laminates

Laminates provide a thin, transparent plastic coating to the surface of printed material such as paperback books, menus and maps. It provides protection from grease and moisture and can be applied single or double sided. This should not be confused with encapsulation.

---

1. Name **two** products that would use the embossing technique. [2]
2. Name a suitable finish to enhance the title on a book cover. [1]

   1. Answers include cards[1] or invitations[1], book covers[1], medicine packaging[1].

   2. UV Varnish[1] or embossing[1] could be used to enhance the title on a cover design.

SHAPING AND FORMING

There are many tools available to help cut, crease, score, perforate and fold.

Steel rule
Measuring, cutting and scoring with a blade or drawing straight lines.

Rotary paper trimmer
To make straight cuts to paper and light card precisely and safely.

Craft knife
General cutting and scoring of various materials.

Scalpel
Fine cutting and scoring. Selection of replaceable blades for different tasks.

Perforating tools
Creates perforations to allow easy folding or tearing off of sections.

Creasing tools
Used like a knife to create a crease. Often made from bone.

Paper shears
Used to cut paper and card. Very long blade for an even cut.

Protractor and compass
Drawing and measuring various arcs and angles.

Rotary cutting wheel
Cuts a line through paper and card. Good for curved cuts.

SCORING, CREASING AND FOLDING

Scoring

Scoring lines on paper only partially cuts through the material, not all the way through. This enables a crisp, clean and flawless fold. Scoring is also used on thicker boards to enable it to fold easily along the scored edge.

Cutting mat
Safe anti-slip, self-healing mat to protect work surfaces.

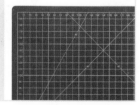

Maun safety rule
The rule has a 'M' profile which keeps fingers away from a knife when cutting or scoring paper.

Creasing machine
Evenly creases the material so it can be folded cleanly and without cracking.

Die cutting

Die cutters enable simple or ornate shapes to be cut from paper or card. Decorative shapes may be tricky to cut by hand and time consuming to produce in any quantity. A die is metal with a raised, sharp area for cutting. They are made in a variety of patterns and designs.

A sheet of selected paper or card stock is fed into the die cutter. The paper is sandwiched between the base plate and the die cutter. Uniform pressure is applied to cut out the chosen design. The sharp edges of the steel-rule dies cut cleanly through the paper or board. These are particularly popular with makers of greetings card and for craft and hobby use.

Digital die cutting is done by machine that uses a small blade to cut out the shape. Using software, designers can create their own custom design which the digital die cutter can accurately repeat.

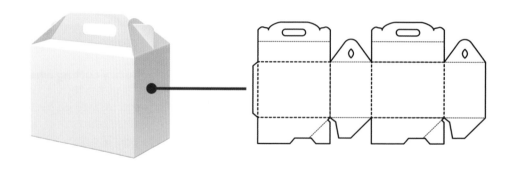

Creasing and folding

Creasing and folding crushes the fibres of paper or board and adds a permanent mark to enable shapes to be formed. This is used in bulk for packaging, creased ready for assembly. Machinery is used for this process to ensure a consistent fold every time.

The ancient art of origami involves folding paper into intricate shapes.

A handmade, 'pop up' birthday card needs an ornate shape cut from the card before it can be folded.

(a) Identify an appropriate tool to cut the shape and justify your choice. [2]

(b) Identify an appropriate tool to crease the card so it can be cleanly folded in half. [1]

(a) The ornate shape can cut with a die cutter[1] which will give a clean and repeatable shape[1]. A scalpel with the correct blade[1] is suitable for low-production numbers[1].

(b) A creasing machine[1] or scoring tool and steel rule.[1]

QUALITY CONTROL

In the mass production of any item, products should be consistent in quality and finish.

Registration marks are printed on the outer edge of a commercially printed item. They are printed using every colour (CMYK) of the four-colour printing process. If the printing is accurate it should overlap precisely so the mark is entirely black. If the colours are slightly out of register or offset, then colour will show.

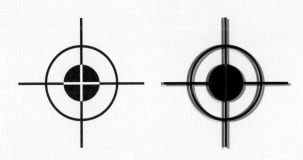

Colour bars are used to measure the various aspects of a printed item such as ink density, overprinting and mis-alignment

SOURCES AND ORIGINS

There are two main types of natural wood – hardwood and softwood. Softwood trees mature more quickly, hardwood trees take longer to grow and replace, making the timber more expensive.

After a tree is felled and cut into manageable lengths, it is then converted into planks. This is known as timber.

Medium Density Fibreboard (MDF)
Waste hardwood or softwood is broken down into fibres and combined with a resin binder.
It is pressed into sheets which are dense and very strong.

Seasoning

Newly cut timber, known as green timber, contains a lot of moisture. In order to reduce the moisture content it should be seasoned.

Air dried timber is separated and stacked under a protective, roofed structure, but with open sides so that air can circulate. This is a slow process.

Kiln dried timber is a quicker process. The kiln is filled with steam, and the moisture content gradually reduced, to dry out the wood. This is a more expensive treatment, but enables timber to be sold more quickly requiring much less storage space.

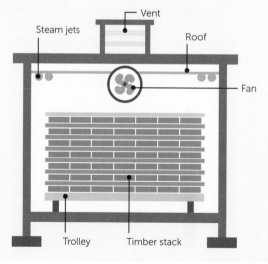

Vent · Steam jets · Roof · Fan · Trolley · Timber stack

Plywood
Thin layers or **veneers** of wood are glued together. Each layer has its wood grain rotated at 90° to each other to produce a composite material that is strong in all directions.

Chipboard
Wood chips of varying sizes are mixed with resin, pressed (to create a strong bond) and formed into a sheet.

Explain **one** way in which softwoods and manufactured boards can be made to look like more expensive hardwoods.   [2]

Boards may be laminated with a thin veneer of hardwood[1] on the outer surface[1]. They may also be laminated with melamine formaldehyde (Formica®)[1] for use as kitchen worktops[1] or stained[1].

PROPERTIES

Designers need to understand the various properties of timbers to select the appropriate type for commercial product manufacture.
Strength, hardness, durability and how easy they are to work with, help a designer select the appropriate material to use.

It is essential to consider the environment in which timber will be used as some perform better for outdoor use than others. **Larch** is durable, hard and resistant to extremes of climate. Its natural oil content makes it suitable for decking, fencing, posts and marine use.

Flat pack furniture

Manufactured boards are commercially used to make flat pack furniture. They are more consistent than natural wood making them easier to work with, drill and cut due to the lack of grain or knots. Board is dimensionally stable so can be transported, stored and assembled with ease.

Advantages

Boards are cheaper than natural woods and can be finished with veneers to give different surface finishes and colours.

Disadvantages

Flat pack furniture chips easily when knocked. It will swell or distort if it gets wet.

Wooden toys

Children's toys need to be durable as they will be dropped, knocked and thrown. As toys are often chewed, they should also resist splintering.

Hardwoods that are hard and durable such as **beech** and **oak** are selected for toy making, as they have a dense grain and can be sanded to a smooth surface or easily painted.

Name a suitable timber for constructing a garden shed and justify your choice. [2]

Larch[1] would be suitable for exterior use as it is tough[1], durable[1], and, due to its natural oil content, it is resistant to water[1].

STOCK FORMS, TYPES AND SIZES

Sizes

Timber is supplied in two main types of finish: **rough sawn** or **planed all round** (**PAR**).

A common size of rough sawn timber is 50 mm × 25 mm. This is used for frame and carcase construction.

Planks, sheets and strips come in a range of stock sizes. Standard practise for measurements is in mm: length × width × thickness. Length × diameter for rod and dowel.

Manufactured board is 2440 mm long × 1220 mm wide. The thickness is usually supplied in 3 mm increments i.e. 6 mm, 9 mm and 12 mm.

Rough sawn timber

Woodscrews

Slotted

Woodscrews join two pieces of wood together and provide strength to a joint. They can also be used to attach locks, hinges and other hardware. They come with different shaped heads for different tasks.

Joining two pieces of wood together using wood screws

Phillips

Woodscrews often need a hole to be pre-drilled through both pieces of wood.

- This is called a pilot hole and should be narrower than the diameter of the screw.

- A clearance hole is drilled into the top section, slightly wider than the diameter of the shank.

Pozidriv®

- If a countersunk screw is being used, the hole should be drilled to the depth of the screw head to allow the screw head to sink just below the surface.

Allen

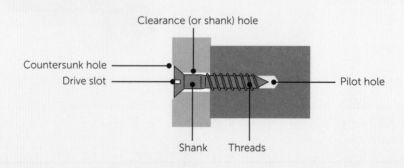

Torx®

Mouldings and dowel

Specially shaped sections of wood are known as mouldings and can be seen around door frames, known as architrave, windows and skirting board.

Dowel rods are circular lengths of timber that are supplied in a variety of diameters. Fluted dowel pins, pre-cut into short lengths are used for wood joints.

Knock down fittings

Flat pack furniture comes with knock down fittings for ease of construction and for easy disassembly. They are intended to be used with simple tools such as screwdriver, drill or Allen key. A connecting bolt or pin draws the two parts of the fitting together to make a strong joint.

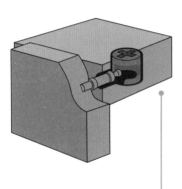

Connecting or block fitting
Plastic corner blocks join two pieces of timber together at right angles. Screws inserted into ready-made holes hold the two pieces together.

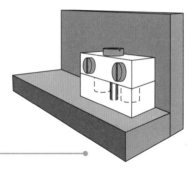

Cam lock fitting
Cam or locking screws come in two parts. The cam, shaped like a disk, fits into a pre-drilled hole in one piece of timber. A connecting screw from the second piece of timber connects with the cam fitting to pull the two panels tightly together.

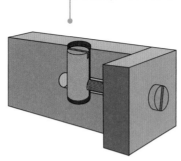

Cross dowel fitting
Also known as scan fittings. A bolt hole is drilled through one piece of wood and into the connecting piece. A dowel hole is drilled laterally across the bolt hole and the cross dowel (metal pin) is slotted in. The two are aligned and the screw tightened to bring the joints together.

Explain why knock down fittings would be suitable for kitchen cabinets. [2]

KD fittings can be easily assembled with a simple selection of tools.[1] They provide a strong enough join[1], are lightweight[1] and can be quickly dismantled without damaging the item[1].

Hinges

Hinges are used to connect two objects together with a pivot on one edge, allowing doors, windows and lids to open and close. They are usually made of steel, brass or plastic.

Butt hinge
Standard hinge used for doors and windows. Needs rebating for a flush fit.

Butterfly hinge
Decorative hinge used in cabinet making and decorative boxes.

Concealed hinge
Used in kitchen cabinets and flat pack furniture.

Flush hinge
Small space saving hinge. Used for lightweight doors and boxes.

Piano or continuous hinge
Provides continuous support along the length of the opening such as large toy chests or piano lids.

Tee hinge
Surface mounted hinge often used on gates or shed doors.

Lamination

Plywood is a manufactured material. A number of thin layers or veneers of wood are laid at right angles to each other. These are glued and heat pressed to create a strong composite. This process is known as laminating. A decorative laminate surface can be added last to provide a protective or attractive surface. This technique is used in laminated flooring materials, office furniture and kitchen units.

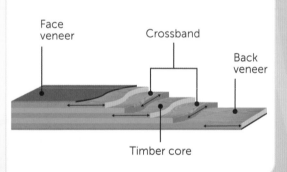

Face veneer Crossband Back veneer Timber core

Laminated timber

Laminated timber or **glulam** is made from strips of wood, layered and bonded together with a strong adhesive. The grain direction runs along the length of the timber. Layers are clamped together until the glue has dried. It produces a strong timber used for load bearing structures such as beams and bridges.

SURFACE TREATMENTS AND FINISHES

The performance of most timbers is improved by the addition of a surface treatment or finish. These can both protect and enhance the appearance.

Oil

Soaks into the timber. As it penetrates the wood it provides protection and some water resistance. It helps replenish a wood's natural oils lost through exposure, age, and wear and tear.

Stain

Permanently stains wood. The colour can be affected by the base wood. It does not protect.

Paint

Applied with a brush or roller. Usually needs a primer or undercoat on bare wood. Paint gives a colour finish and adds a layer of protection against weathering.

Varnish

Varnish is transparent and enhances the natural grain of the timber. Protects from moisture. Varnish can be colour tinted with oil stain. Tends to yellow over time.

Tanalisation

Tantalised timber has been pressure impregnated with wood preservative. It provides a long-term protection against rot, fungal and insect attack. Tanalised timber is used for outdoor applications to extend its life - in particular for fencing, decking, walkways and footbridges. This gives the added advantage that the timber does not need further painting or staining.

Wax

A thin layer is applied with a soft cloth or very fine steel wool and pushed into the wood. This enhances the natural colour and gives a deep shine. Wax helps to protect wood from moisture.

Wood preservative

Protects wood from fungal or insect attack. Helps prevent rot and decay. Will need regular reapplication to maintain levels of protection.

Give **two** reasons why timber might be protected through an additional treatment or finish. [2]

It may be desirable to treat timber to prevent rot[1] and reduce the chance of fungal or insect attack[1]. Timber can have a surface treatment to protect from wear and tear[1] and it can be made easier to wipe clean[1].

SOURCES AND ORIGINS

Metal ores are found in the earth's crust and are obtained by mining. Metals are extracted or separated from the ore and refined ready for use. Metals are extracted by different methods:

Electrolysis

Aluminium is extracted from **bauxite**. The bauxite is purified to produce aluminium oxide. This is converted to aluminium by electrolysis; a process that passes an electrical current through melted aluminium oxide. The pure molten aluminium is separated and collected.

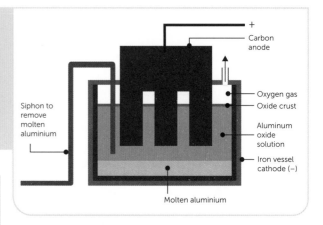

Liquation

Liquation is used with metals with a low melting point, such as tin and lead, to separate the metal from an ore or an alloy. The impure metal is heated inside a sloped container. Once it has melted, the liquid metal runs off leaving behind any impurities.

Blast furnace

Metals are separated from the waste material by heating in a blast furnace. Iron is extracted from iron ore by heating it to around 1700°C until it becomes liquid. The liquid descends through the furnace and separates from the waste ore or slag.

Distillation

Metals such as mercury and zinc have a low boiling point and can be distilled to remove impurities. When mercury is heated, it will vaporise leaving behind the impurities. The vapour is collected and condensed to produce pure mercury.

Refining metals

Refining purifies an impure metal. Different processes are used according to the type of metal, such as fire refining or chemical refining. Electrolysis is also used to separate copper from any impurities.

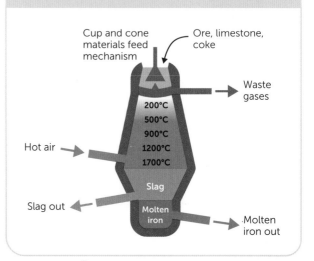

Explain **one** factor that make metal such an energy consuming material to produce [2]

Metal ore needs to be mined from the earth's crust and then processed.[1] The machinery required to extract ore requires significant energy and fuel.[1] Extracting metal from ore requires specialist facilities that consume high quantities of energy[1] for heating or electrolysis processes[1].

PROPERTIES

Metals contain a useful range of properties making them suitable for many commercial products. In selecting a metal, manufacturers must also consider the supply, resulting impact on the environment and the cost of the metal.

Hand tools

Need to be:

- Hard
- Tough
- Resistant to tension and compression
- Ergonomic and comfortable to use

High carbon steel is often used for tool making as it is hard, resists abrasion and high pressure. Chromium may be added to add strength and resist distortion.

Cooking utensils

Need to be:

- Tough
- Durable
- Corrosion resistant
- Food safe
- Flame and heat resistant
- Safe to handle
- Aesthetically pleasing

Stainless steel is commonly used because it is strong, doesn't rust easily and is hygienic.

It is a poor conductor of heat.

Explain why the blade of a chef's knife may require different properties from its handle. [4]

A knife blade needs to be very hard[1] so that it can be sharpened to a fine edge that maintains its sharpness[1]. The handle (or tang) will need to be tougher and less brittle[1] so that it can does not fracture when pressure is applied[1].

Modifying properties of metals

Metals such as steel and cast iron can have their properties altered through heat treatment.

Annealing is the process of heating and slowly cooling a metal to alter its properties, reducing its hardness and increasing ductility. Hard, brittle metals can fracture when bent or pressed. Annealing improves the malleability and reduces the risk of fracture.

Hardening can be applied to steel to improve its mechanical properties. The metal is heated at high temperature which is maintained until some of the carbon content dissolves. The metal is then quenched or rapidly cooled. Hardening increases strength and wear resistance but increases brittleness.

STOCK FORMS, TYPES AND SIZES

Stock form is the form in which a product can be bought and stored ready for use. Designers need to aware of stock sizes in order to manufacture economically and reduce waste.

Standard components

Nuts and bolts are used to join two or more parts together. A bolted joint can be disassembled and reassembled so are important in manufacture. Bolt heads are usually hexagonal for tightening with a spanner or socket set.

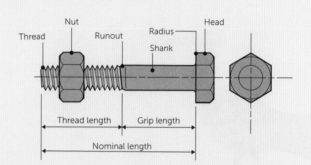

| Hex | Nyloc® | Jam | Wing | Dome | Acorn | Flange | Tee | Square |

Nuts: Usually a hexagonal profile. Used on bolts and machine screws to fasten parts together.

Bolt: Combined with a nut to assemble components together.

Washer: Thin disc of metal to distribute the load on a nut and bolt fastening. Prevents damage to the surface being fixed.

Standard dimensions

Dimensions are given in mm.
Standard dimensions for **sheet** and **flat bar** are given as length × width × thickness.
Box sections and shaped profiles – profile shape plus the length.
Rod – diameter × length. **Tube** – diameter × length plus the thickness of the wall or the gauge.

Angle

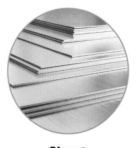

Sheet

Bar

Strip

Screws

Machine screws differ from wood screws by having a finer thread and a parallel shank with no point on the end. They are available in different lengths, diameters and with various head shapes. They are also used as standard components in joining plastics.

Rivets

Rivets are used to join two or more sheets of metal together to create a strong and permanent fixing. Riveting is suited to situations where workers cannot access the back of a product such as in tubing or walls. Rivets are used by the aircraft, shipbuilding and automotive industries, where neatness and strength are important, but also allowing for lighter weight particularly in an aircraft.

They are available in a variety of head types depending on the finish required.

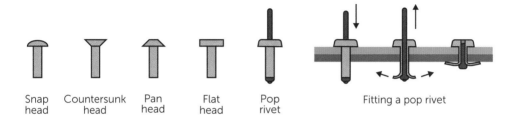

| Snap head | Countersunk head | Pan head | Flat head | Pop rivet | Fitting a pop rivet |

A simple classroom chair is being designed.

(a) Identify a metal stock form for creating the legs of the chair. Justify your choice [2]

(b) Which is the most appropriate nut or fixing to attach the legs to a polymer seat. Justify your choice. [2]

(a) Tube[1] would be suitable as it is strong and lightweight[1]. It can be shaped or bent into the correct form.[1]

(b) A rivet[1] would be most appropriate as it has a smooth head that will not catch on clothing[1] and is not designed to be detached[1]. Alternatively, a low-profile dome nut[1] could be used to attach the legs to the seat without catching on clothing[1], but this may work loose with use.

I-shaped girder   **Tube**   **Rod**   **U-shaped channel**

SPECIALIST TECHNIQUES AND PROCESSES

Metals can be joined together using brazing, soldering and welding.

Brazing

Brazing uses a molten filler, such as brass spelter, to join two surfaces of metals together.

- Enables two different metals to be joined.
- It is a high-temperature process, but a lower temperature than welding for the same base metals.
- The work piece does not melt, just the molten filler, which solidifies when cool.
- Provides a strong joint.

Soldering

Metals are joined with a metal filler known as solder. Solder has a lower melting point than the adjoining metals. Soft soldering is commonly used in manufacturing electrical circuits and plumbing with copper components. Flux is used to help the solder flow and keep the join clean. Hard soldering is used for joining precious metals.

Welding

Welding fuses together metals at a very high temperature.

- The high heat melts the base materials.
- A metal filler (welding rod of the same or similar base metal) is melted to fill the joint.
- As they cool the parts fuse together, creating a very strong join.

Spot welding is a quick process often used to join thin sheets of metal. Automated machines can spot weld to increase speed of production. The weld is not suitable for all purposes as it is small and less strong.

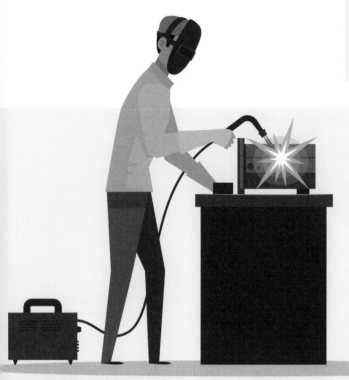

Milling

A milling machine removes metal in thin layers with a rotating multi-toothed cutter. The cutting head can be positioned on one or more axes and set to a specific speed and cutting depth. This is often used for machining parts to a precise tolerance or making a surface completely flat.

CNC milling is highly accurate and usually driven by CAD technology. The high level of control enables complex shapes to be milled, reducing the need for manpower and reducing production costs. Milling is also used for some plastics and wood, especially when modelling.

Bending

A sheet metal former will bend or fold metal sheet or bar to a required shape or bend radius. Thin sheets of metals can be bent cold or cold worked, on a jig or a former.

Casting

Casting is the process of heating metal into its liquid form and pouring it into a mould. The sand-casting process offers the most flexibility and enables complex shapes such as engine parts to be made. Commercial foundries form metal into a multitude of different shapes, sizes, components and parts. Each casting needs a pattern made to precise measurements. This is often produced by CNC machinery.

Pressing

Metal pressing places a flat sheet of metal into a stamping press. With hydraulic force this is pushed into a die to form the shape. This can be a simple mould or a complex mould. Vehicle bonnets and doors are usually pressed.

Explain **two** differences between welding and brazing. [4]

Brazing enables two different metals to be joined but does not fuse them together;[1] welding chemically fuses both pieces together[1]. Brazing happens at a lower temperature than the melting point of the base pieces.[1] Only the filler melts.[1] Welding melts both workpieces together with the filler rod[1]. It is easier to join dissimilar / thinner metals with brazing.[1]

SURFACE TREATMENTS AND FINISHES

Metals need protection from damage and corrosion. Surface treatments and specialist finishes help protect but also improve aesthetics.

Corrosion occurs when the metal reacts with its environment causing an electrochemical reaction.

A surface finish provides an impermeable coating to prevent oxidation. Corrosion can begin when a surface is pitted, or its protective surface is damaged. If the metal is exposed to oxygen and moisture it becomes susceptible to corrosion.

Preparation before adding surface treatments

- Metals must be clean and free of any grease.
- Surfaces can be prepared with abrasive paper.
- Sand blasting is used in industry to smooth the surface and remove debris.
- A primer would be applied to some metals before a final paint finish.

Galvanising

A protective coating of zinc is added to steel or iron to prevent rusting. Zinc is a more reactive metal than iron so if the item is scratched, the zinc reacts first. Hot dipped galvanising submerges the metal in a bath of molten zinc. It is used on gates, pipes, wire, signage and steel frames.

Powder coating

Provides a protective layer to prevent corrosion and for aesthetic reasons. It is applied with a spray gun, giving the particles an electrostatic charge. The metal is grounded which attracts the charged particles. Once coated, the metal is cured in an oven to form a tough bond.

Plastic dip coating

Provides a protective or aesthetic plastic coating onto metal parts such as handles to give a soft, insulative grip. Heated metal is plunged into a fluidised bath of plastic powder. The metal is returned to the oven to allow the plastic to fuse onto it.

Surfaces must often be prepared before adding a treatment.

Explain why a surface should be prepared with abrasive paper, cleaned and free of grease. [2]

A rough surface, known as a 'key' needs to be created using abrasive paper.[1] This ensures that the treatment properly adheres to the surface.[1] Grease and dirt will also prevent adhesion.[1]

SOURCES AND ORIGINS

Man-made polymers are referred to as plastics. Plastics are derived from coal, gas, cellulose and commonly crude oil. Crude oil needs to be processed before use.

Refining crude oil

The process of **fractional distillation** separates crude oil into useful hydrocarbon products. The different components that are separated out are known as fractions. The fractions include petrol, kerosene, diesel and bitumen.

Before the fractions can be used, they need to be broken down by the process of **cracking**.

Cracking breaks large hydrocarbons into individual hydrocarbons called **monomers**.

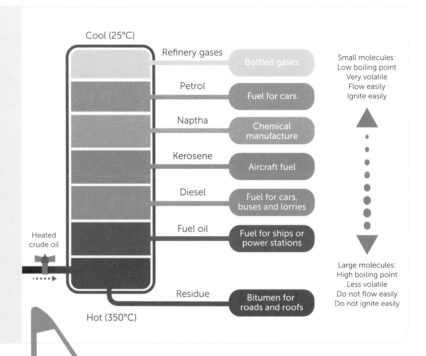

Cool (25°C)

Refinery gases — Bottled gases

Petrol — Fuel for cars

Naptha — Chemical manufacture

Kerosene — Aircraft fuel

Diesel — Fuel for cars, buses and lorries

Fuel oil — Fuel for ships or power stations

Heated crude oil

Residue — Bitumen for roads and roofs

Hot (350°C)

Small molecules:
Low boiling point
Very volatile
Flow easily
Ignite easily

Large molecules:
High boiling point
Less volatile
Do not flow easily
Do not ignite easily

Polymerisation

The individual monomers are joined to form a longer polymer chain. 'Poly' means 'many'. For example, a long chain of ethylene forms **polyethylene** which is used to make carrier bags, toys and bottles.

Explain why crude oil is a finite resource.   [2]

Crude oil is naturally occurring and unrefined[1], formed from the deposits of plants and animals that lived millions of years ago.[1] It cannot be naturally replaced at the rate at which man consumes it[1], making it a limited resource.

PROPERTIES

There are two categories of plastic: **thermoplastics** and **thermosetting** plastics.

Thermoplastics

These are easy to mould and shape when hot. They can be formed into complex shapes and reformed multiple times. They are lightweight, strong, waterproof and corrosion resistant.

- Plastic seating is commonly made from polypropylene
- It has good strength to weight ratio
- It can be injection moulded in bulk
- It can be produced in a variety of colours, style and shapes
- It is easy to clean

Thermosetting plastics

A thermoset is irreversibly hardened and cannot be reformed. It makes a hard, but often brittle plastic which resists deformation. It has good heat and electrical resistance and is commonly used for electrical components, domestic plugs and switches. It also has good chemical resistance and structural integrity. It can be reinforced to produce a strong, durable material.

Modifying plastics

Stabilisers can be added to make plastic more resistant to heat and light. Over time UV light degrades plastic, turning it brittle and faded. This has an impact on strength, and changes the surface appearance and texture.

Pigments can be added to vary the colour of plastics. **Plasticisers** give a material improved flexibility and are commonly used in PVC to improve applications such as sheathing for electrical cables and car interior trim.

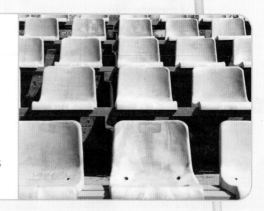

STOCK FORMS, TYPES AND SIZES

Plastics are produced in a range of stock forms, to meet the many uses for manufacturing such as blow moulding, injection moulding and line bending.

Film
Used for packaging, bags, labels and sheeting.

Granules / pellets
Used for extrusion and injection moulding.

Foam
Flexible or rigid. Used for thermal insulation and packaging.

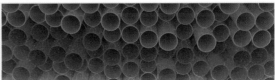

Rods / tubes
Used in electrical, plumbing, garden, military and medical applications. Can be bent to shape.

Powder
Mixes well with additives and dyes. Also used in resin glues, spray coating and 3D printing.

Sheet
Durable and lightweight. Used for protective surfaces, roofing and signage. Can be cut to size, bent, curved or vacuum formed.

Standard dimensions

Dimensions are given in mm.

Standard dimensions for **sheet** are given as length × width × thickness.

Rod – diameter × length. **Tube** – diameter × length plus the thickness of the wall or the **gauge**.

Granules and **powders** are measured by weight in mg.

1. A 1m length of 5mm gauge acrylic weighs 1.4 kilograms. Calculate how much a 400mm length will weigh.   [2]

   1.4 / 1000g = 0.0014
   * 400[1] = 0.56 kg[1]

Standard components

A manufacturer would buy **standard components** rather than making items themselves for improved efficiency and cost.

Metal fastenings are commonly used with plastic; however, they are not ideal for all conditions. The properties of polymer fittings (lightweight and corrosion resistant) make them a suitable alternative to metal in many applications.

Plastic screws, nuts and bolts can be made from PVC, nylon and PET. They possess a range of useful properties:

- Resist corrosion and don't rust, particularly when used in wet or salty conditions.
- Made to be UV resistant.
- Flexible, rigid, lightweight and cost effective.
- Can be reinforced with metal.
- Non-conductive, so ideal for electrical use.

Hinges

Hinges are used to attach doors, windows and lids to frames and carcases. Commonly made from plastic, they can be screwed, glued or welded into position. They resist corrosion and are lightweight. Plastic hinges can be reinforced with glass fibre.

Plastic butt hinge
Polypropylene, lightweight, corrosion resistant, no lubrication needed. Also used in marine, chemical, automotive and aerospace industries.

Continuous hinge
Resistant to solvents, sea water and temperature variation. Alternative to metal piano hinge. Can be cut to size.

2. Explain **one** advantage of using materials that are sold in standard dimensions. [2]

Materials are easier to obtain[1] and likely to be stocked by many retailers[1]. Parts are more likely to be manufactured in large numbers[1], making them cost effective due to economies of scale[1]. Other components will fit with the standard dimensions.[1]

SPECIALIST TECHNIQUES AND PROCESSES

Vacuum forming

  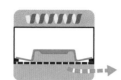

Plastic sheet is placed above the mould and clamped securely

The electric heater is turned on to warm the plastic sheet which becomes flexible

The air is vacuumed out below the plastic and mould

This technique is used to shape plastic. It works by heating a sheet of plastic, which is then pulled by the vacuum to form around the shape or mould. Once the plastic has cooled and set hard it can be removed from the moulding tool.

3D printing

The 3D printing process builds a three-dimensional object formed from reels of thermoplastic. 3D printers use CAD files which are converted into a series of co-ordinates called G-code that the printer will follow to build up the object in layers.

It is also known as additive manufacturing, as the material is added in layers.

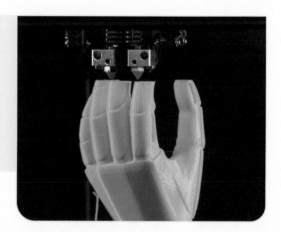

Drape forming

Plastic sheet is heated to a softened state, where it can be formed over a mould. It takes on the shape of the mould without stretching the plastic and retaining the dimensional thickness. It is a slow tool process without the need for a vacuum, so is low cost, but it does take time. It is typically used for components with a gentle curve such as motorcycle windscreens and bath panels.

1. Describe **one** advantage of 3D printing in the home. [3]

New parts can be made as they are required.[1] Well suited to one-off or small batch production[1] of parts for personal needs. Useful to replace parts of domestic appliances.[1] CAD files can be downloaded from the Internet[1] and shared with others[1].

Extrusion

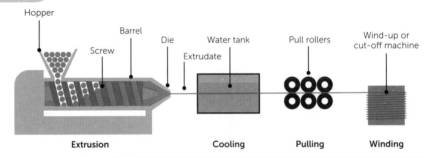

Injection moulding

Products such as bottle caps, toys and automotive parts are produced with injection moulding. Molten material is injected into a mould. Once the plastic has cooled and set hard, the mould is opened to release the shape.

Injection moulding can handle complex parts and shapes to produce consistent products in large quantities.

The process can be automated for a high output rate which helps with cost efficiencies.

This creates a continuous flow of plastic, that is pushed through a die to produce a specific shape or profile. It is used for cables, pipes, mouldings and plastic films for packaging.

Bending

Line bending enables thermoplastics to be folded. Acrylic sheets are suitable for this process.

A line bender heats a sheet of thermoplastic over a strip heater until it is soft. It can then be bent to a chosen angle. When the plastic cools, it retains the shape.

2. State **one** key similarity between extrusion and injection moulding. [1]

Plastic pellets are pushed through a heated barrel[1] using an Archimedes screw[1].

Welding

Plastics can be joined by welding. Heat softens the polymers and they can be joined with a plastic filler material in the form of a long thin cable.

The heat source comes from hot gas welding guns which produces a thin jet of hot air to soften the polymers. Other techniques include laser and friction welding.

Solvent plastic welding can also be used to partially dissolve the plastics, so that they can bond together.

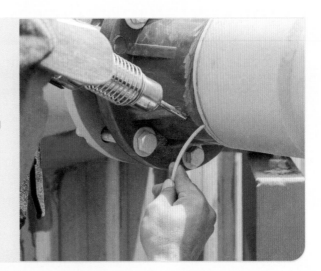

3. A plastic DVD cover needs to be manufactured.
   (a) Identify a suitable moulding process for the cover. [1]
   (b) Give **one** reason for your choice in part (a). [1]

   (a) Injection moulding.[1]

   (b) This provides a consistently accurate shape and form.[1] Mass produced at a low cost per unit.[1]

Resin casting

Resin casting is used for industrial prototypes, precise models and moulds for dentistry. It also a popular with artists, jewellery makers and hobbyists.

Liquid synthetic resin is mixed with a curing agent, poured into a mould and allowed to harden. Unlike extrusion or injection moulding, which forces plastic into a shape, casting relies on gravity to pull the resin in to all parts of the mould.

➕ Resin casting produces a strong final product.

➕ It is has a quick production time.

➖ Its use is limited to smaller scale items.

Blow moulding

A tube of softened plastic, known as a parison is fed into a hollow mould. The parison is pinched at the bottom so it can be filled with warm air and inflates to fill the mould, taking on the shape. This method is used for plastic bottles and containers.

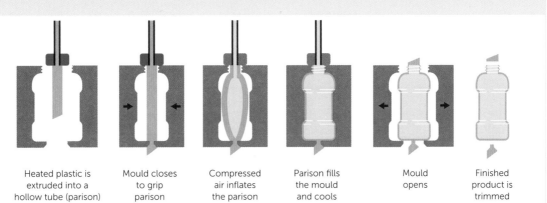

| Heated plastic is extruded into a hollow tube (parison) | Mould closes to grip parison | Compressed air inflates the parison | Parison fills the mould and cools | Mould opens | Finished product is trimmed |

SURFACE TREATMENTS AND FINISHES

Plastics are often referred to as 'self-finishing' in that they are manufactured with their final surface.

Plastics are resistant to decay and corrosion, but their surface may become scratched or dull. Light markings can be restored by using a mild abrasive and a soft polishing cloth. Brasso® can be used to improve the shine of polymers such as acrylic.

Many additional finishes are added for aesthetic purposes.

Designs can also be added to plastic surfaces using offset lithography and flexography.

Plastics can be painted. Before painting, the surface should be prepared.

- It should be clean and free of grease.
- Fine abrasive papers rub down the surface to make it smooth and free of debris.
- A polymer specific primer can be applied.
- Paint suitable for plastics can be sprayed to produce an even finish.

Hydro-graphic printing applies a printed design to a three-dimensional surface. The film containing the design is placed on the surface of water in a dipping tank. The pattern will curve around the surface of the product when submerged.

An acrylic window panel is required for a security booth.

(a) What finishing technique could be used to give one side an opaque appearance? [1]

(b) State the name of a piece of equipment that could be used to achieve this. [1]

(a) Laser etching or engraving.[1]

(b) Laser cutter.[1]

Vinyl-cut decals are printed with a pattern or text onto vinyl with an adhesive backing. They are printed on large rolls and cut using a large format cutter into a variety of shapes. Commonly used on vehicles, window displays and guitars.

Surface treatments for protection

Polymers are affected by exposure to sunlight and UV radiation, and indoor strip fluorescent lighting. The surface of the material takes on a chalky white appearance, the colour fades and the material becomes brittle.

The addition of **stabilisers**, absorbers and **UV blockers** can all slow down the degradation process.

TOOLS, PROCESSES, SHAPING AND FORMING OF TIMBERS, METALS AND POLYMERS

Sawing and cutting

1

Before cutting or shaping, mark out the cutting lines. Measure from a datum point.

2

Material being cut should be securely clamped or held in a vice to prevent movement.

3

Drag the saw backwards to create a nick which marks the starting point clearly. Use the full length of the cutting blade. Avoid pressing too hard.

4

At the end of the cut, support the end piece to ensure a clean cut. Rough edges can be removed.

Wasting is a process of removing unrequired material by cutting sections off or out of a larger piece.

Saws have a blade with a hard, toothed edge. They are used for cutting materials such as timber, plastics and metals to size.

Rip / cross-cut saw

Uses: For cutting wood along or across the grain.

For: Timber.

Tenon saw

Uses: Cutting shallow lines into small pieces of wood. Wood joints.

For: Timber.

Coping saw

Uses: For cutting curved lines through a thin material.

For: Timber, plastic and thin metal.

Hacksaw / junior hacksaw

Uses: Fine toothed for cutting hard materials such as metal and plastic pipes.

For: Metal and plastic.

Jig saw

Uses: A handheld power tool suitable for making straight or curved cuts. It has a reciprocating, narrow saw blade.

For: Timber, metal, plastic.

Sander

Uses: A sander consists of a wheel or pad, covered with abrasive paper. The wheel or pad spins or oscillates rapidly to remove waste material.

For: Timber.

Router

Uses: A handheld router cuts a shape or profile by moving it through the material. **CNC** routing follows a cutting path. The material is secured on a cutting bed so only the router moves.

For: Timber, plastic.

Planer

Uses: For shaping and smoothing by slicing off thin shavings of wood. Planing should follow the direction of the wood grain.

For: Timber.

1. Suggest **one** essential item of PPE to be worn when routing. [1]

   Goggles[1] or safety glasses[1].

Chisels

Wood chisels are hand tools used for carving, chipping, paring and cutting to shape wood. The long blade often has a bevelled edge which is sharpened to give a clean cutting edge.

A carpenter will hit the handle of a chisel with a mallet to create the cutting force. Chisels are made in a variety of shapes and widths to give control for the appropriate task..

Drilling

A drill contains a drill bit, which is the cutting tool. This cuts a circular hole into timber, metal or plastic.

Countersink bit

Cuts a slightly larger hole to allow the head of the screw to sit flush or just below the surface of the material.

Flat bit

Wide, flat blade used for cutting larger diameter holes.

Hole saw

Cylindrical metal blade to cut bigger holes in timber, metal or plastic.

Centre punch

Used on metal to create a tiny mark or dent in the work piece. This helps to guide a drill and prevent drift.

Bradawl

Marking and making holes accurately before drilling or screwing.

Twist bit

General purpose for creating holes in timber, metal or plastic.

Abrading

Abrading scrapes or wears away by friction. Small particles of waste can also be removed by filing and sanding.

Rasp

A coarse file with individual teeth for shaping wood. Produces a rough surface which will need sanding.

File

Hand tool used to remove fine amounts of material. Available in different shapes and coarseness for a range of surfaces.

Wet and dry paper

An abrasive paper with a waterproof backing to allow use with water. Commonly used for paint finishing on metals or to finish acrylic edges to produce a very smooth surface.

Abrasive paper (Sandpaper)

Sheets of paper coated with an abrasive surface ranging from coarse to fine. Abrasive papers are rubbed against a surface to shape and smooth.

Machine tools

Disc or belt sander

A long length of abrasive paper rotates. The machinist can then press a workpiece up against the abrasive surface to sand or to remove thick surfaces such as old paint.

For: Timber.

Band saw

A band saw has a long continuous blade stretched between two wheels. They can be used for very large cuts or with a finer blade for cutting curves and shapes.

For: Timber, plastic and metalwork.

Pillar drill

Pedestal or pillar drills can be floor standing or mounted on a workbench. The drill table is adjustable and a depth stop can be fitted to ensure holes are drilled to a predetermined depth. A pillar drill usually drills at 90°

With its powerful motor it can drill through thick pieces quickly and accurately.

For: Timber, metal and plastic.

Turning

Lathes are commonly used for turning timbers or metals at speed. Whilst the material is spinning, a tool can be held against it to cut, sand and deform evenly around the object. Lathes are used by individual craftsman to produce a variety of components.

Commercial wood turning is operated by **CNC** machinery to produce stair spindles, chair parts, table legs and architectural columns. These components need to be accurately sized and replicated so that they fit perfectly and match others in the final product.

Eye protection should be worn when using a sander to prevent wood chips entering the eyes.

Give **two** other hazards when using a sander and suggest a suitable precaution for each. [4]

Long hair could get caught in rotating parts[1] so it should be tied back[1]. Dust could be breathed in[1] so a dust mask could be worn[1]. Work space may be cramped[1] so other people should not be near the machine at the time[1]. Dust may enter the workshop[1] so extraction equipment should be used.

SOURCES AND ORIGINS

Natural fibres from animal and plant sources and synthetic man-made fibres can be turned into yarn by spinning or twisting. Yarn is then used for producing textiles, knitting, weaving and rope making. Yarn turned into thread is used for sewing.

Natural fibres from animal sources

Silk

Wool

Silkworms spin their **cocoon** which produces a single strand of silk up to 1000 metres long, held together with natural gum. The cocoons are cleaned and softened to remove the gum and unravelled into long threads.

Wool is sourced from sheep, goats, rabbits and camelids. Sheep are shorn to remove their fleece in one piece. The wool is then washed. Wool is naturally curly, so the process of **carding** straightens the fibres which can then be spun into a suitable material for weaving or knitting.

Natural fibres from plant sources

Cotton

Linen

Cotton plants grow in warm climates. The seedpods from the plant are called **bolls**. The bolls ripen and burst open to reveal a fluffy ball of cotton. The balls are harvested, cleaned from the seed pods and the fibres are straightened ready for weaving.

Linen is made from the cellulose fibres that grow inside the stalks of a flax plant. **Flax** is cultivated around the world for its strong, but fine fibres. At harvest, flax is pulled rather than cut. It is left outside to rest and dry, before baling. The fibres are separated from their woody stems to leave the pure fibre.

Man-made fibres

Synthetic fibres are made from raw materials, frequently petrochemicals. These are polymerised to create a long chain or polymer, to produce a variety of synthetic fibres.

Elastane, Lycra® or Spandex

Excellent tensile strength, elasticity and shape retention. Lightweight, fast drying.

Polyamide or Nylon

Nylon fibres are elastic, tough, with good resistance to abrasion yet smooth and soft. Easy to wash and dye.

Polyester

Fibres are strong, elastic, with good crease resistance. Polyester is often spun with other fibres to produce polycotton, which is lightweight, cool and less likely to wrinkle.

---

1. Stretch denim is made from a blend of natural and man-made fibres.

   Give **three** advantages of combining cotton with elastane. [3]

   Cotton is soft and comfortable.[1] It is breathable[1], washes easily[1] and a strong, hardwearing fabric[1]. Elastane is stretchy[1] which makes it more comfortable[1] and increases the ease of movement or fit[1]. Elastane helps material maintain its shape[1] and is crease resistant[1].

2. A horse blanket is made from knitted, recycled polyester fabric.

   Evaluate the suitability of this material for this purpose. [5]

   Knitted fabrics are soft and comfortable.[1] They are flexible[1] and allow movement whilst trapping air between the fibres for warmth[1]. Polyester is strong and hardwearing.[1] It is non-absorbent so will dry quickly once washed or wet.[1] It can be easily cleaned to remove stains, smells and bacteria.[1] Polyester is an inexpensive material[1] and by choosing a recycled material the same properties are delivered with a reduced environmental footprint.[1]

USING AND WORKING WITH MATERIALS

Textiles are highly adaptable materials and can be selected to maximise on the range of useful properties.

Abrasion resistance

Polyester is tough, strong and hardwearing. It is fast drying and lightweight for use in backpacks, sails and tents.

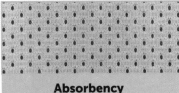

Absorbency

Moisture wicking fabrics, such as polyester or nylon, draw moisture away from the body and dry rapidly, keeping the wearer dry when exercising.

Elasticity

Elastane or Lycra® is exceptionally elastic whilst retaining its shape. It provides comfort and flexibility in sportswear and swimwear. It is hardwearing and quick drying.

Other factors such as durability, comfort, softness and warmth are also considered when selecting a textile for furnishings and homewares.

Acrylic

Properties: Soft, warm, fade resistant, durable. Can be blended with other fibres.

Uses: Carpets, furnishings, soft toys.

Linen

Properties: Strong, durable, creases easily.

Uses: Upholstery, cloths, household linens, and wallpapers.

Cotton

Properties: Durable, soft, warm and abrasion resistant.

Uses: Furnishings and curtains, towelling.

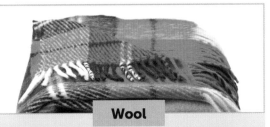

Wool

Properties: Absorbent, soft, strong, renewable and biodegradable.

Uses: Carpets, upholstery, rugs, blankets and insulation material.

MODIFICATION OF TEXTILE PROPERTIES

Flame retardants

Fabrics can be chemically treated to make them more resistant to fire. Fabrics used for upholstery are tested to strict guidelines to ensure they are safe for use in the home or in public spaces. Items sold with a 'fire resistant' label indicate they meet British Standards.

Items protected include:

Children's nightwear	Clothing is treated for their safety, to protect young skin.
Theatre drapes / curtains	Treated to meet strict safety guidelines in public spaces.
Racing drivers' clothing	Treated to protect the driver in the event of an accident.
Protective workwear	Protection from burns for those who work with hot metal e.g. welders.
Furnishings	Sofas, curtains and chairs are all treated to reduce the spread of fire.

Laminated fabrics

Lamination fuses two or more layers of fabric together with heat, adhesives and pressure.

Common uses include: Outdoor clothing and rainwear, outdoor cushions and seating, restaurant seating, car covers, wall coverings and baby bibs.

Protects	Provides a barrier against dirt, grease, liquids and bacteria.
Preserves	Prevents staining, fading and tearing.
Easy to maintain	Provides an easy wipe surface.
Durability	Increases durability and weather resistance. Reduces wear and tear.
Aesthetics	Can improve the surface of textiles, such as blinds and curtains.

Give **two** ways in which lamination can change or improve the properties of fabrics. [2]

Lamination can provide additional surface protection[1], waterproofing[1] insulation[1].

HOW TO SHAPE AND FORM TEXTILES

A textile will be taken from its stock form which can be a sheet or roll, and cut to form a product. Cutting should be accurate to ensure that the pieces of a pattern correctly fit together.

Common cutting tools

Shears or Tailors shears

Used to cut fabrics. The long blades help make cutting straight easier and faster.

Pinking shears

Used to cut material prone to fraying. The zigzag edge can also be used as a decorative finish.

Rotary cutting wheel

Cuts accurate lines and curves on multiple layers of fabric.

Embroidery scissors

Small bladed scissors for delicate work and cutting threads.

Commercial cutting tools

Textile band saw

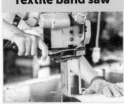

Fast and efficient method to cut out multiple layers of cloth in one pass. Used in commercial settings.

Electric rotary cutting wheel

Speeds up the process of cutting textiles. Used in commercial settings.

Laser cutter

Computer Aided manufacture (CAM) will drive a laser cutter to cut fabric. This is a very accurate and a fast process.

Cutting

A pattern or template will be needed before cutting fabric. This will be pinned to the fabric ready for tracing. The pattern will include a seam allowance. This is the additional amount of fabric needed for seam turning. Pattern markings should be added to the fabric to ensure it is assembled correctly.

SEWING

Sewing joins fabrics together or fastens objects using a needle and thread. It can be performed by hand or by using a machine. Hand sewing is very useful for fine, delicate work, small repairs and restoration. **Machine sewing** is quicker, stronger, and in some cases, neater.

There are many types of stitches used in sewing, suitable for practical purposes or a decorative finish.

A seam joins two pieces of fabric together. A **plain seam** gives a flat finish and is not visible on the correct side of the product. The edges of a seam should also be finished to prevent **fraying**. An **overlocker** trims off any surplus fabric and covers the seam edge with looped stitches.

Running stitch (straight)

A basic stitch that is quick and easy to produce. Often used to tack cloth together before creating a seam. The finished stitch gives a dashed line effect.

Back stitch

As the name suggest, this stitch loops back over itself and is more durable than the running stitch. The finished stitch gives a solid line.

Chain stitch

Chain and looped stitches are mainly used for decorative purposes. The stitch tension should be kept quite loose so as to keep the shape of the stitch.

Blanket stitch

Traditionally used on the edges of fabrics such as fleece to give a durable edge. It helps prevent fluffy strands coming away from the edges. There are a number of decorative varieties of blanket stitch.

Zigzag stitch

The zigzag stitch can be used to reinforce areas prone to stress such as around buttonholes. It is also good for sewing fabrics that are stretchy. It can help prevent fraying by enclosing the raw edge of fabric.

Overlock stitch

The overlock stitch is created with a machine called an overlocker. It is used to create a durable edge, hem or seam over one or two pieces of cloth and used particularly in garment construction. An overlocker is faster than a standard sewing machine and can hold more reels of thread.

PLEATING, GATHERING AND QUILTING

Fabrics can be shaped and manipulated with pleats, gathering and tucks to give added shape.

Pleating

Box pleat

Knife pleat

Accordion

Pleating adds folds to a fabric to create volume and texture, increase ease of movement and add strength. Pleats are formed by doubling fabric back upon itself and keeping it in place. Pleats can be pressed or heat-set into shape, or sewn into place.

Gathering

Gathering is another sewing technique to manage the fullness of a fabric, and to create shape. It may be used at a waistband, on cuffs or on shoulder pieces. It is also used on curtains to create a series of folds in the length of fabric, so it hangs well.

Quilting

Quilting is a process of sewing several layers of fabric together to form a thick and warm structure. It is usually made up of a decorative top layer, wadding for thickness and warmth, and a simpler backing material. A variety of stitches are used for strength to hold it all together and for decoration. The top of the quilt can be created from patchwork patterns and embroidery.

Piping

Piping forms a trim to define the edges of cushions, upholstery and some garments. It is formed by folding a strip of fabric over a length of piping cord and sewn along the edge. The fabric is cut along the bias to make it easier to bend around corners and prevent puckering.

Give **two** disadvantages of pleating. [2]

Pleating will require additional material which will add to the weight[1], production time[1] and material cost[1] of a garment.

STOCK FORMS, TYPES AND SIZES

Rolls of fabric

Fabrics on a roll are usually sold in standard widths of 90cm, 115cm and 150cm. The length of the roll may vary.

Ball of yarn

Wool or yarn may be sold by ball, skein or hank. It is sold by weight.

Reels of yarn

Reels of yarn are generally used for machine production. The reels are produced in variety of lengths. The thickness of the fibre is measured in ply. 2-ply is two twisted strands, 4-ply is four plied strands.

Zips

Consists of two rows of interlocking teeth which are opened or closed with a slider.

- Used to fasten openings on fabrics such as bags, jackets, jeans and sleeping bags
- Made of metal or plastic.
- Secure, hardwearing, can be washed.

Buttons and toggles

Made of plastic, wood, metal or horn.

Sewn on and fastened with a buttonhole or loop.

- Can be made to match the fabric.
- Can be replaced.
- May fall off or be damaged in the wash.

Press stud or popper

Pair of interlocking discs often made of metal or plastic.

Provide quick fastening on shirts, coats, bags and purses.

- Hardwearing.
- Washable.
- Secure fastening device.

Velcro®

Consists of two components. One side covered with tiny nylon hooks, the other covered with tiny loops.

When pressed together, the parts fasten securely. An adjustable and reusable fastening.

- Hardwearing and washable.
- Used on children's clothes and shoes.
- Practical, but not aesthetic.
- Velcro® needs securely attaching as it is pulled each time it is opened.

COMMERCIAL DYEING PROCESSES

Dyeing changes the colour of a fabric and can also be used to add a pattern.

Dyes

Natural dyes

Natural dyes are produced from plants, invertebrates and minerals. Natural dyes produce a diverse range of rich and complementary colours. However, the colour may vary slightly with each batch. They are not dependent on non-renewable resources and don't produce toxins.

Synthetic dyes

Synthetic dyes produce long lasting and consistent colour results. They are made from chemical resources and petroleum by-products. Some of the chemicals used are toxic and can be harmful to people and the environment. Waste-water from the dyeing process needs to be carefully processed.

Commercial dyeing

The **commercial dyeing** industry dyes large volumes of fabrics that are used for producing household items and clothing.

Continuous dyeing: Large quantities of raw fabric on long rolls are machine fed through tanks or troughs of dye. It's a time- and cost-efficient method of producing large batches of the same colour. The fabric is steamed or dry heated to fix the colour. It is then washed, dried and wound ready for delivery.

Batch dyeing: Batch dyeing enables a smaller quantity of fabric to be dyed a specific colour. It enables manufacturers to respond quickly to a request for a particular colour. The fabric is passed back and forth through a tank of dye until the colour is fully used up or exhausted. The fabric is fixed, washed and dried.

Stock dyeing: Before fabrics are spun or woven, the fibres can be dyed. The loose fibres are put into large vats containing the dye. This is heated so the dye molecules are absorbed by the fibres, until the desired colour is obtained. For weavers, this gives more control over colour.

Hand dyeing

With **hand dyeing** methods, natural fibres such as cotton or linen take dye well.

Resist dyeing: Resist dyeing prevents dye from reaching all of the cloth. It's a traditional method of hand dyeing. Batik is a wax resist dyeing technique that originated in Indonesia. Hot wax is used to mask an area of the fabric in a decorative pattern using a tool called a tjanting. When the fabric is dyed, the wax resists the dye. When the fabric is washed to remove the wax, the undyed area reveals the pattern.

Tie-dye: Once known as tied and dyed, this method consists of twisting, folding, crumpling the fabric and holding it in place with string or elastic bands. When the cloth is dyed, the folds and bands act as a resist and prevent the dye from reaching all of the fabric.

PRINTING

Screen printing

Screen printing is a popular method of hand printing a design onto fabric. It is a low-cost option for small print runs and commonly used for t-shirt design.

- The screen is a wooden frame with a fine mesh fabric stretched across it.
- The chosen design or text is set into the mesh with a layer of light reactive emulsion which hardens under bright light, producing the desired stencil.
- Printing ink is poured over screen and pressed through the fine mesh to create a printed design on the fabric.

➕ It is an effective, low cost option for creating striking designs with vibrant colours.

➖ Screens and stencils can take time to make and each colour layer is applied separately.

Flatbed screen printing

Flatbed screen printing uses several screens at once. The fabric is laid firmly in place along a conveyor, the screens are lowered onto the fabric and the ink applied. The fabric will be programmed to move along the conveyor a controlled length at a time.

Rotary screen printing

Rotary screen printing is the most frequently used commercial method as it allows for continuous production. A cylinder is used instead of a screen, and each cylinder applies a single layer of colour. Ink reservoirs pump the ink through the inside of the cylinder. As it rolls along the fabric, a squeegee pushes the ink out in controlled amounts.

> PrinT make bespoke T-shirt designs using digital printing.
>
> Explain **two** advantages and **one** disadvantage of digital printing to PrinT.[6]
>
> *Advantages include: Quick and easy to produce one-off products due to very short setup times.[1] Photo-realistic images are easily achieved[1] so it can produce prints that are not possible with conventional methods.[1] Low labour costs.[1] Can save designs electronically[1] which can be retrieved for re-orders of popular designs[1].*
>
> *Disadvantages include: Initial costs for the machinery are high.[1] Print quality can be less durable or hardwearing.[1]*

Sublimation printing

Sublimation printing applies sublimation inks onto fabric using a combination of heat and pressure. Dye based inks are printed on to sublimation paper. The paper is laid on to the fabric and heat pressed. The heat turns the inks in the paper from a solid to gaseous state which then penetrate the fibres of the fabric. Polyester fibres are most suitable for this process as the heat makes the pores of the material open to full absorb the inks.

SURFACE TREATMENTS

Fabrics can have a finishing process applied that will improve their performance, functionality or enhance the aesthetics.

Block printing

Block printing uses ink dipped blocks made of wood or linoleum that are pressed onto fabric.

- The pattern is cut into the block leaving a raised design which takes the ink.
- ⊕ It gives complete control over hand printing the design.
- ⊕ Design can be easily repeated, and colours changed.

Digital printing

This is an ink-jet form of printing using textile inks for printing onto fabric. Rolls of fabric are fed through a printer and the ink is applied to the surface in the form of thousands of tiny droplets. Heat or steam is then used to cure the fabric and ensure the inks are set.

- ⊕ More complex and intricate patterns can be produced using graphic design software for printing onto fabric.
- ⊕ Small runs of fabric can be printed, adopting a lean or just-in-time method.
- ⊕ It enables designers to react to trends and fashions which are often short lived.
- ⊖ Setup and equipment costs can be high.

Weaving

Weaving interlaces two sets of yarns at right angles to form fabric. The **warp** threads run the length of the fabric and the **weft** threads run across the width. There are many different types of weave; **plain** and **twill** are very common.

Modern textiles are produced on large scale industrial looms which are often computer controlled following CAD designs. Increased automation helps produce consistent and fault free textiles with a faster rate of productivity.

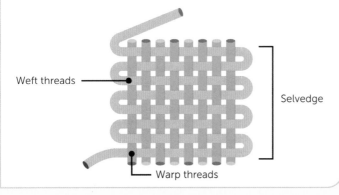

Stain protection

Adding stain resistance is a chemical process which prevents water or oil-based spills from attaching themselves to the fabric and affecting the colour. This is often used on carpets, furnishings and shoes.

Water repellency

Silicone based chemicals can be added to fabrics to provide a durable water repellent barrier.

Mould and rot protection

Waterproofing can also help protect against mould and rot. A PVC coating on textiles protects against mould, which can cause fabrics to rot and disintegrate. Heavy duty canvas can be treated to be rot and water resistant and have a flame-retardant finish.

Printing

Die-cut decals can be produced on specialised film or papers for heat transfer onto cloth. These can make striking and individual designs for all forms of apparel, bags and textiles.

Embossing

Fabric can be passed through heated, decorative rollers that will press a pattern into the texture of the cloth.

USING AND WORKING WITH MATERIALS

Electronic and mechanical systems are made up from a variety of materials, selected for their properties that make them suitable for the different uses. By improving the properties offered by a system, the performance can be enhanced.

Motor vehicles

Technology has changed many aspects of our lives. The automotive industry is continually improving systems and innovations. Embedded controllers in our cars are constantly monitoring functions we take for granted such as engine temperature, air temperature, fuel injection, transmission, ABS and airbag to name a few. Developments in manufacturing, by using lightweight and recycled materials, contribute to increased efficiency and end of life recovery of cars today.

Designers are continually developing:

- **Hybrid engines and electric vehicles**
  Hybrids and electric vehicles have improved fuel efficiency, reduced CO_2 emissions and are travelling further for less cost.

- **Autonomous vehicles**
  Developments in collision avoidance systems, data capture and sensors to understand what is around the body of the car are constantly being improved to enable vehicles to make real-time decisions as they navigate our roads and traffic systems.

- **Wi-Fi and connectivity in cars**
  Satellite navigations systems are included in many cars as standard. Other communication systems are being incorporated to automatically feedback information in the case of a breakdown or to monitor wear and tear.

- **Head-up display (HUD)**
  Projects key data onto the windscreen just into the driver's line of sight. This may include speed, simple mapping, fuel gauge and distance to the vehicle in front.

Domestic appliances

Design of domestic appliances has developed considerably to improve the functionality as well as the aesthetics. Items need to be able to withstand repetitive use, be durable and hard wearing or with hand appliances, more lightweight. Developments in technology have enabled designers to incorporate systems to make appliances more energy efficient.

Appliances, such as washing machines or dishwashers can be programmed to function in a certain way. By incorporating a microcontroller, which contains its own internal clock, a series of processes can be programmed to control the appliance.

- A switch can start the washing cycle.
- A thermistor will regulate the temperature of the water.
- A buzzer may indicate the cycle is complete.
- LEDs are used for indicator lights.

By improving electronic control systems, additional features can be added to further improve functionality such as detecting the weight of a load, a delayed start function and door release timing.

Anodising aluminium

The properties of aluminium can be modified by the process of anodising. This is a process of electrolysis which makes the surface of the aluminium oxidise, converting the metal surface into a hard, durable, corrosion resistant finish. Aluminium can also be dyed during the anodising process which adds to the aesthetics and means the colour doesn't peel or chip off. It also adds a level of electrical insulation.

It is used in parts for aircraft, vehicles and shipping as well as in electronics such as smartphones.

Discuss how bus transportation has evolved through the addition of new technologies.

Your answer may include developments in passenger comfort, ticketing and bus design. [6]

Passenger facilities may now include the use of Wi-Fi on board and thinner seating design providing additional legroom. Bus tracking services can accurately indicate waiting times. Ticketing facilities may now include wireless NFC communication with mobile phones and contactless bank cards. Buses are now using hydrogen, biofuels and electric motor technology. This can make buses quieter and helps the environment. This question is assessed using the levels of response table on page 145.

SHAPING AND FORMING

Solder is used to connect two or more contacts so that electricity can flow between the components in an electrical circuit. This can be applied manually by melting the solder with a soldering iron, or using production line machinery.

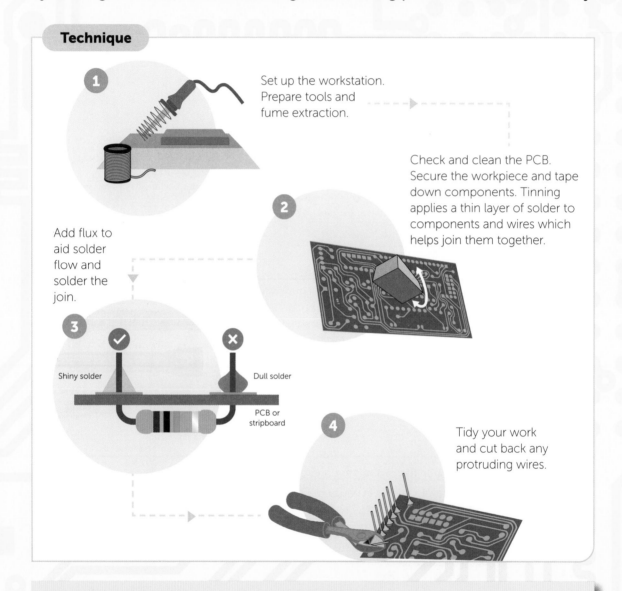

Technique

1 Set up the workstation. Prepare tools and fume extraction.

2 Check and clean the PCB. Secure the workpiece and tape down components. Tinning applies a thin layer of solder to components and wires which helps join them together.

Add flux to aid solder flow and solder the join.

3 Shiny solder   Dull solder

PCB or stripboard

4 Tidy your work and cut back any protruding wires.

Explain **two** safety issues to consider when using a soldering iron. [4]

Risks include burning from the heating element or tip of the soldering iron[1], a melted or damaged cable or plug[1] and the risk of electrocution[1]. You should hold the soldering iron by the polymer handle only[1] and always use the stand to prevent accidental contact[1]. The cable and plug should be PAT tested to ensure that it is in safe working order.[1] Silicon rubber shielding on the cable is resistant to a much higher temperature than normal insulation and can withstand melting.[1] A low voltage iron will reduce the risk of electric shock.[1]

Printed Circuit Board (PCB) manufacture

A PCB connects electrical components using conductive tracks and pads. They are made from photoresist board, a glass reinforced polymer with a thin layer of copper laminated onto it. Etching is the process commonly used to create the circuit in the layer of copper.

The etching process:

- Using computer software, the circuit is drawn, and a mask printed on to clear acetate sheet.
- Copper coated, photo resist board is cut to size and the light resist backing removed.
- The acetate mask is placed onto the board and the board exposed to UV light, causing a chemical change in the photo resist layer.
- The board is washed and then placed in an etching tank which removes the excess copper.
- Only the copper tracks protected by the mask will remain. The board is washed again and is now ready for drilling and soldering.

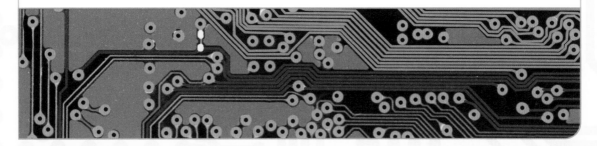

Cutting

Printed circuit boards can be cut using a precision guillotine. The cutting bed is often fitted with a ruler to enable accurate cutting.

Using CAD, a laser cutter can be used to cut out complex shapes in a circuit board.

Laser cutters direct a very powerful laser beam at a precise focal length to cut or etch the chosen material. The beam burns through the material to produce a very clean cut or fine engraving.

Drilling

The pins and wires of components being placed on a PCB need to be pushed through small holes and soldered in place.

For accuracy when drilling these holes, a specialist drill bit is required between 1mm and 1.5mm diameter.

A drill mounted on a stand helps with accuracy and ensures straight holes.

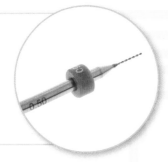

Machining PCBs

A model of a circuit is drawn using computer software. Using a CNC milling machine, software will identify the areas of copper to be removed mechanically. This avoids the use of chemicals. Drilling can also be completed as part of the machine process.

STOCK FORMS, TYPES AND SIZES

Current and voltage

Current	Voltage
This is the rate at which an electric charge flows in a circuit. This is measured in amperes or **Amps** (**A**).	**Volts** (**V**) is the potential difference or the electrical force that drives the electrical current between two points.

Mains electrical power in most countries is between 220 and 240 volts.

Household appliances and electrical items have a voltage rating close to the supply. If the voltage rating is too high it could cause the item to fail. Too low and it may not work.

Standard components

Integrated circuits (**IC**) are small self-contained circuits. An IC takes the form of a **dual in-line package** (**DIL**) A rectangular block of plastic with two parallel rows of connecting pins. Most DILs are connected to a PCB by inserting their pins through holes and soldering them in place. Each of the pins on a DIL IC are commonly spaced by 0.1" (2.54mm).

Microcontrollers are supplied in many forms and are also known as **peripheral interface controllers** (PICs). They are often sold as DIL packages that can be programmed to carry out a range of tasks. They contain memory and run at a voltage of between 3 and 5.5 V.

Give the value of the resistor shown in the diagram opposite.[1]

10k +/- 10%[1]

Resistors

Resistors are passive components that restrict the flow of electricity in a circuit.

They can be used to lower the voltage within a circuit.

- Resistance is measured in ohms Ω (a single ohm is a very small unit).
- A resistor has a series of coloured bands on its body.
- Each band represents a different value.
- To work out the value in ohms, refer to the colour chart.
- Read the colours from left to right.

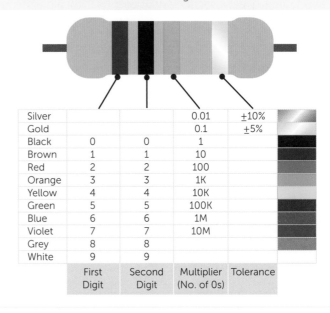

	First Digit	Second Digit	Multiplier (No. of 0s)	Tolerance	
Silver			0.01	±10%	
Gold			0.1	±5%	
Black	0	0	1		
Brown	1	1	10		
Red	2	2	100		
Orange	3	3	1K		
Yellow	4	4	10K		
Green	5	5	100K		
Blue	6	6	1M		
Violet	7	7	10M		
Grey	8	8			
White	9	9			

COMMERCIAL PROCESSES

Soldering robots are used in industry. The process is fully automated and programmed to produce precise and repeatable results.

Pick and place assembly

Commercially manufactured PCBs use surface-mount technology. Components are mounted directly onto the surface of the PCB. **Pick and place machines** are robotic machines which are used to place the components, many of which are extremely small and difficult to place manually. This system of component placement is very quick and completed with a high level of precision.

Manufacturers will set up quality control systems to check at regular stages throughout production that the boards have been correctly assembled and meet quality guidelines.

Flow soldering

A solder paste, made from powdered solder and flux, is used to temporarily attach electrical components to their contact pads. The board is then heated making the paste melt which then flows, creating a solder joint. This method of flow soldering is used to attach surface mount components to a circuit board. Heating is done carefully with either an infra-red lamp, placing the board in a reflow oven or by warming individual components with a hot air pencil.

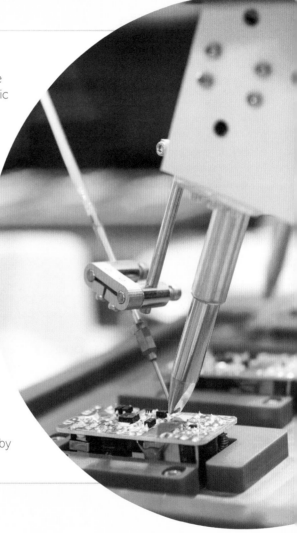

Give **two** benefits of pick and place technology over hand assembled boards [2]

Pick and place machines are precise[1], quick[1] and able to work with tiny components[1].

SURFACE TREATMENTS AND LUBRICANTS

Surface finishes

Printed circuit boards are used in many items for the home, industry, and in environments that maybe damp, dusty or exposed to extremes of temperature. If PCBs are left unprotected, they may deteriorate and oxidise making the board unusable.

A lacquer, known as an acrylic conformal coating, can be sprayed onto a PCB for surface protection. It is fast drying and fluoresces under UV light making it easier to check during **quality control**.

Lubricants

Applying a substance such as grease or oil to mechanical components provides smooth movement, minimises friction and reduces wear and tear. A thin layer of liquid between two surfaces stops them rubbing together, prolonging their working life.

Resistors are given an aesthetic finish that also performs an essential function.

(a) State what finish is given to resistors. [1]

(b) Explain why this finish is given rather than numerical labelling. [2]

(a) Paint[1] and lacquer.

(b) Coloured bands are easier to see than small text labels[1] which would be hard to read.[1]

SCALES OF PRODUCTION

Different methods of production are used depending on the type of product being produced. Methods are also influenced by quality and quantity.

Batch

Companies use batch production to make consistent products, maintaining a quality standard. Examples of batch produced goods include clothing, baked goods, newspapers and electrical goods.

- Products can be produced in large batches, reducing the overall cost per item.
- Templates or moulds can ensure consistency of production.
- Each batch will be tested for quality and uniformity.
- Machinery may need to be recalibrated or stopped between batches causing downtime.

Prototype

A prototype is a representation of a product before it is produced in any quantity. It helps evaluate and test a design, and to confirm design methods and costs.

One-off production

One-off production is the manufacture of a single item. This may be a custom or bespoke item made specifically to a client's brief. The build quality and level of skilled craftsmanship will be high, but the cost of production will also be high. Examples include a hand-made wedding dress, a cruise liner or a piece of jewellery.

Wet

Oil

Used in motorised vehicles to reduce heat, friction and wear.

Grease

A form of oil with a thickener ensures it remains in contact with the moving surfaces. It doesn't leak and remains in place.

Dry

Graphite

Graphite is a form of carbon that is very soft and reduces friction. It is used as dry lubricant as it has no sticky residue that can attract dust.

Molybdenum disulfide

A silvery-black compound that is used as a solid lubricant. It provides lubrication in instances of high pressure, load or temperature.

Mass production

This is the manufacture of standardised products in large quantities. Vehicles, pharmaceuticals, popular soft drinks and mobile phones are all mass produced.

- Automation of processes and assembly lines contribute to the efficient manufacture of high-volume products.
- Automated assembly line production requires fewer workers.
- The set-up costs for efficient automated machinery or robots can be high.
- The cost advantage of producing high volumes of products means the costs are spread over a large number of goods manufactured, reducing the cost per unit.

Continuous production

A continuous process that takes place 24 hours a day, 7 days a week. Continuous production is used for manufacturing many household chemicals, petrochemicals, cement and steel for example.

- Industries using continuous production are very expensive to run.
- Oil refinery, blast furnaces, power stations, paper pulp production, smelting and chemical manufacture are all continuous processes.
- Processes will be highly automated with a small work force.
- Machinery is set up to produce large volumes of one item.

Discuss the benefits of a bespoke or tailor-made suit compared to a buying an off-the-peg suit in a department store. [4]

A bespoke suit is made to fit an individual client.[1] It will be measured, patterned and cut to ensure a perfect fit.[1] It will meet the client's specification in terms of fit, drape, detail and design.[1] A bespoke suit is commonly made from high-quality fabrics[1], which can be expensive. The result will be better quality than a ready-to-wear suit.[1] It needs to be made by a highly skilled tailor.

SPECIALIST TECHNIQUES AND PROCESSES

Production aids

A manufacturing or production aid is any device, tool, template, jig or pattern to help improve the speed and accuracy of the production process. More detail on page 131.

Jigs

Jigs are used to hold a piece of material during cutting, drilling or bending.

- Jigs improve accuracy and efficiency
- Secure the work piece quickly and without causing any damage to the material
- Work piece is always located against a reference point or datum edge.

Templates

Templates are shaped pieces of material used in cutting, drilling and shaping. Templates ensure that an item is accurately made and can be replicated to ensure a consistent quality. For repeated use they should be made of a durable material.

Paper patterns

Paper patterns are often attached to a material to be cut such as in textiles or laying out shapes to be cut in wood or card.

Measurements and reference points

Accuracy is important to achieve a quality, finished product. Measurements can be taken with a simple ruler or tape measure. Protractors can be used to measure angles when used with a ruler or a T-square. French curves enable curves to be drawn in different sizes.

Datum reference point

A datum **reference point** is the point from which all measurements are taken. A single datum point is often found in the corner of a design or from the centre or edge of a circular shape. Accuracy is increased by ensuring measurements are taken from only these points.

In computer aided manufacture (CAM), the machinery is aligned to a point where the X- and Y-axis meet. This method of measurement enables sizes to be accurately scaled up or down.

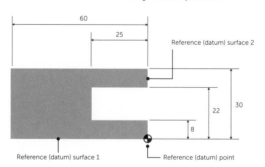

Scale drawing

A **scale drawing** allows a designer to accurately represent an object or building in a more practical size. The diagram will include accurate measurements that have been enlarged or reduced by a specified amount known as a **scale**. The scale factor will be shown on the drawing, for example 1:5. When something is drawn to scale it gives a clear understanding of the proposed shapes and spacial relationships.

EXAMINATION PRACTICE

*These are questions that can be answered through the knowledge and application of **ANY** chosen material area.*

1. Five materials are listed in the table below. Select **one** of the materials:

Foam board	Cedar	Brass	Lycra	Acrylic sheet

   (a) State **one** method that can be used to join your chosen material. [1]

   (b) Give **one** property of your chosen material. [1]

2. Describe **two** different forms of stock materials, giving examples in your answers. [4]

3. Select **one** of the following materials below.
   - Polyethylene terephthalate (PET) – for use in water bottles
   - Foil backed board – for use in takeaway food container lids
   - Copper – electrical cable
   - Beech – for use as children's toys
   - Cotton – for use as a shirt
   - Photo sensitive printed circuit board (PCB) – for use as circuit board for a night light

   Give **two** ways in which the material is shaped or formed during the manufacture of the product. [2]

4. Identical products are often produced on a production line.

   Explain what is meant by the each of the following terms in relation to the scale of production. Give examples in your answer.
      (a) Batch [2]
      (b) Mass [2]

5. Name **two** different primary sources of materials. [2]

6. Wasting is a subtractive process.
      (a) Explain what is meant by the term wasting. [1]
      (b) State **one** chosen material and give **two** different school-based wasting processes for your choice. [2]

7. Name **two** different commercial processes that could be used to cut, shape or finish materials. [2]

8. For one material area, describe a process that can be used to improve a material's resistance to stress. [2]

9. Surface treatments can improve the function or aesthetics of a product.
      (a) Explain **one** functional reason for applying a surface treatment or finish. [2]
      (b) Explain **one** aesthetic reason for applying a surface treatment or finish. [2]

10. Quality control checks include measurable and quantitative systems to check products during the manufacturing process.

   Using a product of your own choice, discuss how the manufacturer uses quality control checks during the manufacturing processes. [6]

11. Choose **one** product in Figure 1 and describe **two** features or reasons that make it suitable for batch production. [4]

| Summer dress | Cast iron cookware | Floating bath toy |
| Wooden pepper mill | Valentines card | Christmas lights |

Figure 1

12. Choose **one** of the following materials.
   - Urea formaldehyde – for moulded electrical fittings
   - Bleed proof paper – for drawing rendered designs with marker pens
   - Stainless steel – for kitchen utensils
   - Oak – for a child's toy box
   - Cotton – for a bed sheet
   - Buzzer – for use in a door entry system

   (a) Give **two** different reasons why its functional and/or aesthetic characteristics are suited for the intended use. [4]

   (b) For **one** of the materials listed above, name **one** of the primary sources it is made from. [1]

   (c) Name **one** process used to convert the raw material into the workable form selected above. [1]

SECTION C
3.3 DESIGNING AND MAKING PRINCIPLES

Information

At least 15% of the exam will assess maths and at least 10% will assess science.

All dimensions are in millimetres.

The marks for questions are shown in brackets.

The maximum mark for this paper is 100.

There are 20 marks for Section A, 30 marks for Section B and 50 marks for Section C.

Specification areas 3.3.1 to 3.3.11 are covered in this Section. Some content has been covered in other sections where it relates more closely to the materials or techniques covered.

INVESTIGATION, PRIMARY AND SECONDARY DATA

Designing to meet needs, wants and values can improve people's lives in many ways. Poor design can achieve the opposite effect.

A wide range of information and decisions need to be covered as part of the process.

Investigation

Before and during the design of a product, designers and manufacturers need to understand the needs and wants of the consumer.

Market research

Before a product is made, market research helps a designer understand whether there is a target market. They will gather opinions and comments from consumers about their interest in the new product.

Primary market research collects research data first-hand for a specific purpose. It is created by those needing the data.

Secondary market research gives access to information created by others. There are vast amounts of secondary market research data available to access.

Primary data sources

- Interviews
- Questionnaires
- Surveys
- Focus groups
- Case studies
- User observations
- Product testing and trials

Advantages

- Data is up to date and relevant.
- Questions and surveys can be tailored to specific needs.

Disadvantages

- A large number of people are needed.
- Data gathering is time consuming.

Secondary data sources

- Government data
- Articles from books, magazines and the Internet
- Company reports
- Exemplar work from others

Advantages

- Data is already collated and available.
- Data may be free or low cost.
- Huge amount of research is available and accessible.

Disadvantages

- Data may not be up to date.
- Data may not be specific to company needs.
- Data is available for all.

Designers need to identify the information they must gather before beginning any primary market research.

Examples of data gathered during market research

Define the target market

- Who is the product aimed at?
- Age group
- Gender
- Lifestyle, hobbies and interests
- Socio-economic group

Information needed

- Do consumers already buy this type of product?
- Is there a need for another?
- Do they like the style/design/colour/texture?
- How much would they pay for it?

There are different ways to gather information:

Methods of data gathering for market research

Interviews

- Conducted face to face or over the telephone.
- Answers can be more detailed.
- Interviews can be recorded.
- Takes longer to summarise the feedback.

Focus groups

- A group of people brought together to share feedback.
- Researchers can listen and observe body language and reactions.
- More time to give in-depth answers.
- Small focus groups are easier to control and keep discussion on topic.

Questionnaires

- A series of questions on a paper- or Internet-based form.
- Could include rating style questions i.e. excellent, good, fair, poor.
- Closed ended questions – only a yes or no answer.
- Open ended questions – requires a written answer.
- Some may not provide enough detail or an honest appraisal.

Product analysis and evaluation

Researching and understanding existing products on the market, analysing how they function and their commercial success, are key steps for designers to encompass before beginning their own work. Products will be critically analysed to consider the following:

Function	Form	Ergonomics
Aesthetics	Materials used	Cost and retail price
Sustainability / environmental impact	Customer feedback and recommendations	Manufacturing process

ERGONOMICS

Ergonomics is the process of designing products and workplaces to fit the people who use them. It improves the human interaction with a product, environment or workspace, and minimises the risk of injury.

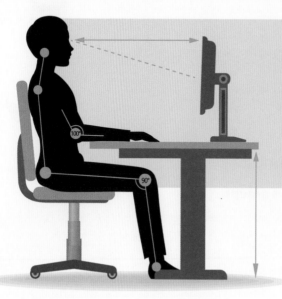

Many people sit for long periods of time at a desk.

If the height of the computer, chair and desk are not correctly aligned to the user, it can cause pain and **repetitive strain injury**.

Designers will consider the measurements of humans and products to ensure they function well together.

Anthropometric data

Anthropometric data is the study of the human body, its measurement and proportions.

Data will be collected from a large sample of people of a variety of sizes to gather detailed body measurements.

Weight measurements are also taken to understand the stress or load a component may need to withstand.

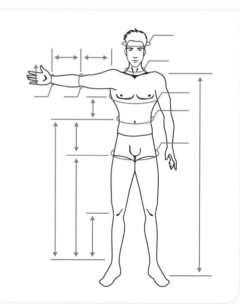

Explain **one** way in which ergonomics can aid carrying a product. [2]

The design of ergonomic handles will make carrying a product more comfortable.[1] A form-fitting design will help evenly distribute the load through the fingers.[1] The inclusion of hand holds in boxes or in large bulky items will make lifting easier and safer.[1]

Holdalls, rucksacks and baby carriers can be designed to fit the body with adjustable straps and belts[1] to spread the load more evenly and reduce strain[1].

Percentile graph

Products are often designed to fit the majority of the market. There will be a small number of people who will fall outside the average range.

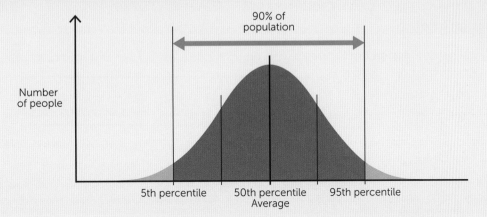

Percentile ranges used in anthropometrics and ergonomics

The graph could indicate that 90% of people will fit the height of the desk opposite.

5% are too short, 5% are too tall so the desk design will not work so well for them.

Presentation of research and data

Data should be presented in a format that is logical for a designer to interpret and act upon.

Qualitative data provides an insight into thoughts, opinions and is often expressed in words.

Quantitative data generates numerical or measurable data or data that can be used in statistics.

Bar charts or pie charts	Useful methods of presenting quantitative data.
Spreadsheet	Calculating and presenting cost and sales forecasts.
Graphs and charts	Show trends and patterns in data.
Video and audio	Demonstrate feedback and reactions from focus groups and interviews.
Documents and reports	Summarised data with key areas highlighted or a transcript from a recorded interview.

DESIGN AND MANUFACTURING

Designers work through a series of steps during the **design process** to ensure a new product satisfies the consumers' needs or wants.

Design brief

A designer needs a **design brief** to begin work on a new idea. This is often provided by a client and they will outline their expectations:

- The product and its purpose
- The target market, who will use it
- Budget and timescale
- Where it would be sold
- How and where it would be used

Once an idea or design has been developed it will go through further analysis and **market research** to help develop the design and identify any problems.

The findings and conclusions are presented to the client. This stage of the process is crucial as the investigation and research may suggest that the design concept needs rethinking or may not be worth producing at all.

Design specification

Once the brief is agreed, a design specification can be drawn up which includes more product detail.

Design specification content

What	A clear description of the product and its function or purpose.
Who	The target market, age range, gender.
Why	Need in the market has been identified and how it will meet this.
How much	Estimated costs.
How long	Timescale to manufacture.
Materials and aesthetics	Choice of materials, colour, texture, finish.
Environment	Selection of materials for recycle and reuse, sustainability.
Safety	International standards and safety requirements met.
Measurables	Dimensions and weights.

Modifying a design brief

Specification checks, research and analysis continue throughout the design process, in order to identify any unexpected issues or problems and resolve them as soon as possible.

During testing of a prototype, designers may discover errors in dimensions, that a material isn't strong enough or a selected finish isn't hard wearing enough. Adjustments or changes in methods will need to be made and the earlier this is done, the less impact it will have on time and cost.

Manufacturing specification

A manufacturing specification is a document containing all the information needed to make a product. The document will include technical drawings or CAD diagrams, process flowcharts and timing plans.

Examples of content in a manufacturing specification

Assembly	Information on components, parts and how they fit together.
Annotations	Explanation of elements of design that may not be obvious from the diagram.
Equipment	Machinery or specialised equipment needed for manufacture.
Materials	All materials needed and their manufacturing processes.
Quantities	Materials and component quantities required and batch numbers.
Dimensions	Accurate and appropriate specifications (e.g. in mm, weight, density) with tolerances.
Quality control	QC checks, what needs to be checked and how often.

Write a design brief for **one** of the following six products.

Your answer should consider four of the following points: Purpose, target market, use, measurements, safety, the environment and aesthetics. [4]

Coffee cup – *to safely, securely and hygienically hold hot liquids[1] without leaking or allowing oils to penetrate the casing.[1] Suitable design for adults.[1] The lid should use eco-friendly bioplastics.[1] Insulative sleeve to protect from heat[1] and a secure lid design to prevent the spill of hot liquids.[1]*

Bread bin – *to provide a container to fit at least one standard loaf of bread[1] with a good seal to make it airtight[1]. Designed for homeowners.[1] Made from sustainable timber with a protective finish.[1]*

Toolbox – *to provide a lockable box for tools storage.[1] Requires a secure carry handle[1] designed to be comfortable to hold[1] and take the weight of the contents[1]. A finish that protects it from rust and knocks.[1] Long enough to hold a large hammer.[1] Wide enough to contain several tools.*

Desk tidy – *to provide easy access to a range of compartments to store pencils, sharpeners and paper clips.[1] Suitable for 11+.[1] Made from a recyclable polymer[1], with smooth edges and curves.[1]*

Luggage strap – *to secure suitcases whilst travelling[1] and provide identification of the bag[1]. Needs to be long enough to fit around a large bag capable of holding in excess of 23kg of baggage allowance.[1] Practical for travellers of all ages.[1] Strap and buckle must be strong enough to pick up the suitcase by the strap only.[1] Use of vivid colours and design for easy identification.[1]*

Wind-up toy – *entertainment suitable for young children of age 3+.[1] Must avoid the use of small parts that could be swallowed.[1] Needs to use a wind-up mechanism to simulate the movements of chattering teeth whilst it moves or jumps around.[1] Should be able to withstand knocks and drops.[1]*

ENVIRONMENTAL, SOCIAL AND ECONOMIC CHALLENGES

Environmental, social and economic challenges influence design. Responsible designers and manufacturers are continually looking at how to reduce their use of limited resources and use new technologies to meet with consumer demand.

Fair trade

Fair trade aims to offer improved terms of trade to local producers and workers. By buying fair trade goods, it helps to support local communities, who can afford to develop and improve their methods of production. See page 4 for more detail.

Many farmers cannot compete with highly subsidised producers and will be offered poor rates for their products. Fair trade organisations give farmers an alternative route to market and ensure a higher and stable income.

Textile designers can source fair trade cotton which is often grown in an ethical and environmentally friendly way. This helps countless workers who work in the cotton farms in developing countries.

Explain the impact of deforestation on the greenhouse effect. [3]

Trees absorb carbon dioxide[1], offsetting the greenhouse gases produced by humans[1]. The act of deforestation produces additional greenhouse gas emissions.[1] The removal of trees takes away the vegetation crucial to absorbing carbon dioxide.[1]

Deforestation

Deforestation is the permanent removal of trees and clearing the land for agricultural use and grazing. The timber may be used for fuel, construction or manufacturing. There are many effects of deforestation including contributing to global warming.

Designers can rethink the way they source and use materials.

The Forest Stewardship Council® (FSC) certifies materials which are sourced from sustainably managed forests. This means the forest will use selective logging and replanting to create a cycle of productivity that doesn't harm the forest environment.

Increased use of recycled paper and timber materials avoids more trees being felled.

Changes in energy sources and methods of manufacturing can also help manufacturers reduce their carbon footprint and impact on global warming.

THE WORK OF OTHER DESIGNERS

Researching designers and products provides a greater understanding of the materials and processes they used. It can also help inspire new ideas.

Harry Beck
1902–1974

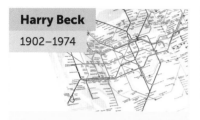

Harry Beck was a technical draftsman who visually simplified the layout of the London Underground by producing a clear and simple map layout of the tube system. He transformed the way people navigate around London's underground network and his design has influenced many other underground maps around the world.

Norman Foster
1935–present

Award winning British architect known for his striking architecture and high-tech vision. His practice 'Foster + Partners' are known for the Millennium Bridge, Great Court at the British Museum, City Hall, 30 St Mary Axe (the Gherkin) in London, Reichstag in Berlin and a host of other buildings around the world.

Marcel Breuer
1902–1981

Modernist designer and architect, known for two of the most iconic chairs of the 20th century, the tubular steel Wassily Chair and the cantilevered Cesca Chair, which he designed at the **Bauhaus**.

Sir Alec Issigonis
1906–1988

Designer of the Morris Minor and of the ground-breaking Mini, which used unconventional design features including a transverse engine with front wheel drive.

William Morris
1834–1896

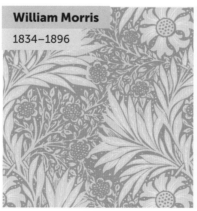

Coco Chanel
1883–1971

French designer, founder of the Chanel brand. Known for introducing a more casual feminine line of clothing, breaking away from corsets and long skirts.

Alexander McQueen
1969–2010

British Fashion designer renowned for his unconventional designs and stunning catwalk shows combining sharp tailoring with theatrical design.

William Morris was a significant contributor to the British **Arts and Crafts Movement**, Morris is renowned for his block printed fabrics and wallpapers. His designs were influenced by nature with beautiful patterns of intertwined flowers, leaves and birds.

Dame Mary Quant

1934–present

Famous for bringing the mini skirt to popularity along with her shiny raincoats and 'paint box' make-up. Her geometric mod style epitomised the sixties fashion era.

Charles Rennie Mackintosh

1868–1928

Architect and designer who played a formative role in the **Art Nouveau** movement. He was commissioned to design a new building for the Glasgow School of Art which became his masterwork.

Raymond Templier

1891–1968

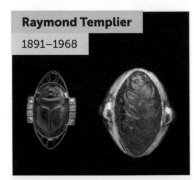

Templier came from a family of traditional jewellers, but his jewellery designs used bold geometric shapes with precious stones mounted into metals such as platinum and silver. He became an influential figure in the **Art Deco** movement.

Aldo Rossi

1931–1997

Italian architect and product designer of the **Post-Modern** movement. Produced iconic artefacts for Moteni and Alessi and recognised for his contributions to architectural theory.

Ettore Sottsass

1917–2007

Sottsass set up an architecture and design studio in Milan in the 1940s. He worked as a design consultant to Olivetti and helped revamp the bland styling of office equipment with the 'Valentine' typewriter in 1969. He founded the '**Memphis Group**' which was known for its postmodern furniture and decorative pieces.

Louis Comfort Tiffany

1848–1933

Tiffany was an American decorative arts designer, renowned for his highly decorated, stained-glass lamp designs which became an icon of the **Art Nouveau** movement.

Gerrit Rietveld

1888–1964

Dutch architect and furniture designer. His work used a simple, primary, colour palette with an abstract composition. His work was characteristic of **De Stijl**, a **modernist** art movement.

Philippe Starck

1949–present

French designer, Starck has produced many iconic products such as the Juicy Salif, as part of his collaboration with Alessi. His designs are innovative, sleek with a touch of humour and often use organic forms. His designs include household items, furniture and interiors.

Dame Vivienne Westwood

1941–present

British fashion designer renowned for establishing punk and new wave clothing in the 1970s. Her non-conformist approach to design is exuberant with decadent tailoring that is often designed to shock.

THE WORK OF OTHER DESIGN COMPANIES

Alessi

Founded by Giovanni Alessi in 1921 originally producing metal tableware. Alessi expanded into producing many household items, collaborating with industrial designers such as Aldo Rossi, Ettore Sottsass and Phillipe Starck. Their products are recognisable for the use of colour, and fun design.

Apple

An American technology company that best known for its designs of personal computers, the iPhone and portable media players such as the iPod, Apple Watch and Apple TV. Their ethos of combining stylish design with a great user experience has made them the world's largest technology company, with a high level of brand loyalty.

Braun

Max Braun started the company in Germany in the 1920s producing radios and record players. His product design was renowned for simplicity, but with a high level of user friendliness through to the smallest detail. Braun's range expanded to include shavers and other household appliances.

Dyson

In 1978 James Dyson made improvements to the traditional vacuum cleaner. Five years and 5,127 iterations later he developed the first bagless cleaner. Dyson Ltd is now a global technology company producing household products with quality and functionality at the top of its agenda.

Gap

Founded in 1969 selling jeans and records, Gap is now a global fashion business selling their distinctive range of casual clothing in 90 countries. Denim, and their classic 5 pocket jean is still at the heart of the business with a continual focus on attention to detail, comfort and design.

Primark

The first clothing store opened in Dublin in 1969. There are now 360 stores worldwide. Their range now includes shoes, beauty products and homewares. It operates at the low-cost end of the market for shoppers seeking the latest fashions at modest prices; known as a 'fast fashion' brand.

Under Armour

Founded in 1996 in America by Kevin Plank, an American football player who was tired of having to change out of the sweat soaked t-shirt worn under his jersey. He developed a moisture-wicking synthetic fabric that keeps athletes cool and dry. From this lightweight fabric, Under Armour was born and it is now a global brand with a range of performance apparel.

Zara

Zara is a Spanish clothing retailer founded by Amancio Ortega in 1975. With over 2,000 stores worldwide Zara leads in fast fashion with its highly responsive supply chain. Its efficient design, production and distribution business model enables Zara stores to receive new designs weekly.

DESIGN STRATEGIES

Collaboration

The process of working with others to create something. It is a human activity, bringing people together to pool ideas and concepts, to be developed into a final solution. Companies may use a range of designers or collaborate with other successful designers to create a special edition or limited range. This often happens in the fashion industry.

User centred design (UCD)

At each stage of a design process, designers need to focus on the user and their needs. Development of a design takes into account the user's requirements, objectives and their feedback. UCD involves the user through a series of research and investigative steps to make a usable product.

Systems approach

A systems approach considers all the steps in a process or project and how they affect it. The system as a whole is analysed, rather than individual steps. This often uses flowcharts, block diagrams and other visual methods to represent the various stages of a system or sub-system.

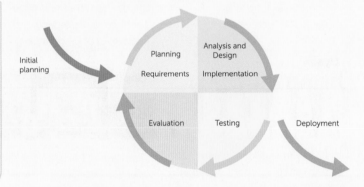

Iterative design

Designers use the iterative process to continually improve a design or product. It's a continual cycle of prototyping, testing, gathering feedback and making improvements until a final product is ready for release.

Advantages

- Ensures a product is fit for purpose.
- Meets functionality requirements.
- Is reliable and usable.
- Cost saving process preventing manufacturing with errors.

Avoiding design fixation

Design fixation stops a designer considering multiple strategies to solve a design problem or develop a new idea. Designers can become stuck on a single idea and need to use a range of techniques to challenge their own thinking and generate new designs.

Give **one** method of non-destructive testing. [1]

X-ray imaging[1], leak testing[1], radar[1], electromagnetic testing[1], acoustic emission testing[1].

Explore and develop ideas using sketching, modelling, testing and evaluation

Sketching

Sketching ideas are an important first step to get a concept onto paper. Early ideas can be roughed out, edited and developed. A more detailed final sketch can show a design concept in detail with dimensions and material choices included with annotations.

Modelling

Taking an idea from a sketch into a model is a low-cost method of seeing how a product looks and works. Models can be produced with CAD or made by hand to scale.

Working models can be made of a cheap material to check proportions and dimensional accuracy.

A mock-up of a garment is known as a **toile**. Calico is a durable, but low cost fabric that is used for toiles and can be marked with a pen to indicate adjustments and changes.

A **breadboard** is a solderless, re-usable board for prototyping electronics.

The dimensions, aesthetics, ease of use and material choice can all be evaluated by producing a model. 3D printing is also suitable for making prototypes quickly and with accuracy.

Testing

Testing is an ongoing process throughout design and manufacturing.

- Data should be gathered throughout the process.
- The results can be evaluated to help determine the best idea to take forward.
- The sketching, modelling, testing and evaluation process continues until a design meets all the criteria.
- A prototype can then be produced.

Destructive testing	Non-destructive testing	Market testing
Tests a product to its extreme. Data gathered helps guide a manufacturer on the appropriate choice of materials and construction method.	Identifies areas of weakness. Tests the function and usability without destroying the prototype or end product.	Looks at how the product performs with user groups and client testing. Their feedback is analysed.

Evaluation

Evaluation informs a designer about which parts of a product work and which need improving.

- Recording the results from testing is a key step in the design process. Results should be logged at each stage as it enables the data to be evaluated.
- Products will be evaluated at each stage of their development against the list of criteria laid out in a design specification.
- Designers will also evaluate against other products to become aware of their competition.

COMMUNICATION OF DESIGN IDEAS

Freehand sketching

Freehand sketching can be used to present an idea in a graphical form. It's a method of drawing without measuring instruments or drawing aids and can be a quick way to get initial ideas down on paper.

The addition of colour, texture and shading all enhance a sketch and help to communicate the design concept. Marker pens can be used to add a colour wash and shadows.

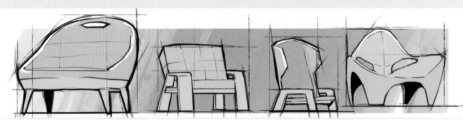

Give **one** advantage of drawing in perspective. [2]

Drawing in perspective enables designers to represent three dimensional images[1] on a two-dimensional plane. With the use of vanishing points, perspective drawing shows what something may look like in relation to surrounding objects.[1] Designs appear as the eye would see.[1]

Isometric projection

Isometric drawing enables a designer to draw an object in three dimensions, but without using perspective.

- All vertical lines stay vertical.
- Horizontal lines are drawn at 30° to the horizontal plane.
- Isometric graph paper helps with accurate drawing.
- Measurements can be taken from isometric drawings.

One-point perspective

A method of drawing that shows the view becoming smaller as it gets further away and converges at a single vanishing point. This type of drawing is suitable when the object is viewed straight on.

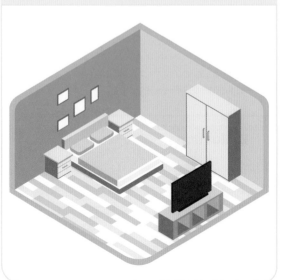

2D and 3D sketching

Two-dimensional design is useful for plan views, showing dimensions.

Three-dimensional design helps show how it may look and feel to be in a room.

Systems diagrams

Systems diagrams visually explain the order of events in a mechanical, electrical or electronic system. Blocks represent the different stages of a system such as its inputs, processes, decisions and outputs.

In project planning, a systems diagram helps to simplify the steps and clearly communicate each required process. The systems approach is covered in more detail on page 120.

Schematic design

Schematic diagrams are representations of a system. In electronics, symbols are simplified to represent the components such as a resistor or switch. A **circuit diagram** is a schematic which shows how components connect.

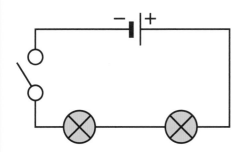

In the fashion industry schematic diagrams are referred to as **flats**. It clearly outlines the technical details of a garment but does not show a body. Although many are hand drawn, industry standard is to produce digitally drawn diagrams with symmetry, clean lines and true to life proportions.

Exploded diagrams

Exploded diagrams show the constructional detail and assembly of a product. The components are shown separately and each part in proportion to each other.

The diagram shows parts which may be hidden from view once assembled. This helps with fitting a product together such as assembling flat pack furniture.

Explain why exploded drawings are commonly used for the home assembly of furniture. [2]

The diagrams show parts which may be hidden from view once assembled.[1] This helps to clearly see how a product fits together[1] helping to form a logical layout and aid planning the construction[1].

Annotated drawings

Annotations or notes add details and explanations to a design.

Labels can indicate:

- Choice of materials
- Specific detailing
- Fixings and fastenings
- Tolerances
- Colours and patterns

Mathematical modelling

Mathematical modelling is used as part of the iterative design process. It's an important step as it helps inform and predict the behaviour of a device or system being designed.

- Graphs and charts can inform about aspects of the design.
- Simulation and predictions can be calculated and displayed.
- Performance can be evaluated and compared.
- Clients can see how mathematical calculations have been applied in the design process.
- Ergonomic and anthropometric data can be gathered in a spreadsheet or database.
- Results from focus and test groups can be collated.

Audio and visual recording

Design work can be supported with audio and visual recordings. They can be used to gather:

- Interviews with user groups and the client to determine needs.
- Feedback on a design.
- Recordings of a focus group to see and hear how they react to a product.

Video can also be used to demonstrate how a product works or to record destructive / non-destructive testing.

Photographs of each stage of development provide useful visual data for reference.

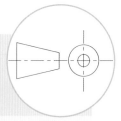

Working drawings

Working drawings contain dimensional and graphical information that can be used to work to or assemble a component. A working drawing, referred to as an orthographic drawing, has three main views: a plan view, front and side view.

Orthographic drawing conventions

The common format of a working drawing is a **third angle orthographic projection**, drawn accurately and to scale to give a manufacturer a clear overview of a design.

Dimensions will be shown in mm.

A symbol to indicate it's a third angle orthographic projection will be shown.

Outlines	——————
Construction lines	————
Centre lines	— · — · —
Dimension lines	◄————►
Hidden details	— — — — —

Scale and dimensions

A drawing of an object will have its real sizes enlarged or reduced by a certain amount or specified **scale**. Scale must be clearly shown on the drawing.

The scale shown on the drawing will represent the **drawn length : actual length.**

Scale is represented as a ratio for example:

1cm to 1m	=	1 cm : 1 m
	=	1 cm : 100 cm
	=	1:100

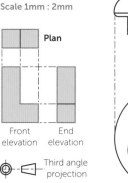

Scale 1mm : 2mm

Plan

Front elevation

End elevation

Third angle projection

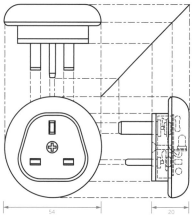

54   20

Dimensions should show the actual dimensions of an object, not the dimensions of a drawing. Measurements are shown in millimetres (mm).

CAD modelling

Computer aided design replaces manual drawing with an automated process. It is used by designers, architects and engineers to produce technical and precision drawings. It can produce two-dimensional or three-dimensional diagrams which can then be rotated so that a design can be viewed from any angle.

Prototypes are often constructed based on prior models. Describe how modelling can be used by designers to help develop prototypes. [4]

Prototyping enables a 3D impression to be created to improve visualisation.[1] It can reduce development time[1] and can avoid excessive use of materials[1]. Early testing using computer-based modelling such as CAD or circuit design can be used.[1] Physical models using card, a toile or breadboards can be created using materials that are significantly cheaper than the actual finished material.[1] Moving components and mechanisms can be tested.[1] Electronic models can be shared and worked on collaboratively by several parties who may not be in the same room or country.[1]

PROTOTYPE DEVELOPMENT

Development of prototypes

A prototype is an early stage model of a product. It will be developed for a client to check that it meets their requirements.

Satisfying the requirements of the brief and client requirements

The design brief will contain all the details about the product and should be referred to in the prototype development as a reminder of the client's wants and needs. If issues arise in the making of the prototype, corrections can be made to the product specification.

Prototype functionality

A prototype should be made so that it is able to demonstrate how it works and show it is suitable for its intended purpose.

Aesthetics

A product should function as expected, but good design and finish are also important. Aesthetics involves all the senses. Touch, vision, hearing, taste and smell all affect a user's response to an object. Prototypes should demonstrate the intended finish.

Marketable

A new or improved design should produce a marketable product. If a product works well and looks good, it should be attractive to its target audience.

Evaluating prototypes

A prototype must also be rigorously tested to ensure it:

- Meets all the design criteria
- Is fit for purpose
- Meets all safety criteria
- Follows the manufacturing specification

All of these findings will be recorded and evaluated.

In order to get the best out of the testing and evaluation process, designers should:

- Reflect on their own design, test and use it to see that it meets the criteria set out.
- Be able to analyse client and user group feedback.
- Recognise and make the changes or modifications that may be needed.
- Clearly assess that the prototype is fit for purpose.

EXAMINATION PRACTICE

1. Give **three** different methods of gathering primary research. [3]

2. Explain **one** disadvantage of using secondary research. [2]

3. Explain **one** reason why products are designed to meet the needs of 90% of the population. [2]

4. Give **two** key features a design brief should contain. [2]

5. Explain **one** reason why consumers buy fair trade products. [2]

6. Using **one** of the companies in the list below, discuss the key features of their work. [4]

Alessi	Apple	Braun	Dyson	Gap	Primark	Under Armour	Zara

7. Explain what is meant by the term 'collaborative design'. [2]

8. Give **two** advantages of using orthographic projection as a form of communication [2]

9. Explain **two** reasons for evaluating the prototype of a model. [4]

10. Give **three** different mathematical modelling methods. [3]

11. Explain **one** advantage of destructive testing. [2]

12. A kitchen table is sketched below.

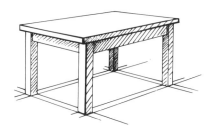

(a) Identify the drawing style used. [1]

(b) Ergonomics and anthropometrics are commonly used when designing products such as the table.

    (i) Define what is meant by 'ergonomics'. [2]

    (ii) Suggest and justify how **one** anthropometric data measurement may have been used in the design of the table. [2]

SELECTION OF MATERIALS AND COMPONENTS

Designers need to consider a range of factors as part of their selection process for materials and components.

Availability

- Are the chosen materials available in stock forms?
- Are expensive or rare materials needed that are harder to source?
- Does the supply of materials affect the production flow?
- Have the materials been sourced from a renewable supply?
- Have the raw materials been processed without causing environmental damage?

Functional need

Functionality is vital in product design. Designers need to consider:

- Will the selected material function as expected?
- Is it strong enough? Will it resist wear and tear?
- Does it need to be weatherproof or chemically resistant?
- Is the product safe?
- What standards does it need to conform to?

Cost

- Does the cost of manufacturing meet the expected budget?
- Does the selected production method (mass, batch or one-off) impact the cost of materials?
- Are bespoke sizes required?

QUALITY CONTROL AND TOLERANCE

In the mass production of any item, products should be consistent in size, quality and finish as well as being safe and effective for use. **Quality Control (QC)** is an essential stage in manufacture.

Accurate working

When working with papers and boards, accurate length and width measurements are important to check. The weight and thickness of the stock is also key, as it may affect the manufacturing process or final use. For instance, a greetings card should fit the appropriate envelope, or a poster must be the right size for its frame. Bank notes are printed to very specific dimensions and weight, as any variation helps detect fraudulent notes.

Tolerance

Tolerance is the amount of error allowed for a given task. It is applied to distance measurements and weights such as in fabric, paper or card. There will be a specified measurement range which is an acceptable difference in size between an upper limit and a lower limit.

Resistors and capacitors in electronic devices have tolerances which need to be considered when trying to calculate how a circuit or system may perform. Resistors have coloured stripes which denote their specific resistance value.

- During a making activity, it may not be possible to achieve 100% accuracy.
- An appropriate degree of tolerance needs to be considered for a given product or component.
- This could vary from a fraction of a millimetre to a few millimetres.
- A narrower tolerance is usually required for more technical elements e.g., metalwork, wood joints, 3D printed or laser-cut components, aligning fabrics or specific levels of voltage required in a circuit.

Go/no-go

A go/no-go gauge is used to check dimensions are within specified tolerances. The expected dimensions and tolerances will be pre-set. For instance, when checking a drill hole, if the go gauge fits but the no-go gauge does not, the hole is within tolerance.

Depth stop

A depth stop ensures a hole will be drilled to the correct depth. The limit is set to control how far the drill bit enters the workpiece. This is an integral part of a pillar drill or can be in the form of cap added to a power or hand drill.

Metal band saws can also be fitted with an adjustable stop to ensure a blade only cuts to a pre-set depth.

Laser settings

Laser cutters direct a powerful laser beam at a precise focal length to cut, etch or engrave the chosen material. This includes plastics such as acrylics and ABS, metals such as aluminium, wood, glass and stone. It is an accurate process as the laser beam does not blunt or wear out. The speed, power and dimension settings must be set according to the material. High power and slow speed is suitable for cutting, however laser cutting consumes a lot of power.

Seam allowance

A **seam allowance** is the area between the line of stitching and the edge of the fabric. Commercially, a seam allowance may only be 10 mm to save on fabric (15 mm with home sewing). The tolerance is very small, so accurate stitching is needed otherwise pieces will not fit as intended.

Dimensional accuracy

Textiles with a repeated pattern such as florals, stripes or checks need constant **quality control** checks to ensure the pattern repeats accurately vertically and horizontally. Although many checks are made by eye, machine vision systems are being introduced to scan and detect physical or pattern defects. This automated process is extremely fast, but the computer equipment is costly, so it is only used by large scale factories at present.

Timings with printed circuit boards

Printed circuit boards (PCBs) can be made using the photo etching process. This process corrosively etches away selected areas of sheet metal. It is a precise process which can produce complex circuits with fine detail.

The steps of cleaning, UV exposure, developing, washing and etching need specific timing to ensure the exact results are met. If the exposure times or etching times are too long, it will remove all of the copper causing broken tracks; too short and unwanted copper may remain on the board causing short circuits.

Commercially finished etched boards are inspected both visually and by machine.

Explain the purpose of 'quality control'. [2]

Quality control checks or tests a product to ensure that it meets pre-set standards, tolerances or specification criteria.[1] It guarantees the accuracy of a part or component[1] and that it is fit for purpose, and of an acceptable standard for sale[1].

TEMPLATES, PATTERNS AND JIGS

Templates, patterns and jigs are used to ensure repetitive accuracy when marking out and cutting out materials.

Templates

A template is a specific shape that can be drawn or cut around. For a one-off production, a paper template may be used. When batches of identical shapes are needed, a template would be made of a more durable material to withstand repeated use.

Patterns

Patterns are used in textiles and for casting.

A sewing pattern is a **template**, often made of paper or a lightweight cardboard for repeated use. It is made up of several pieces which represent the different sections of a garment. The outline is marked onto the fabric which is then cut out and assembled. The outline may be traced by hand or with CAM.

A pattern can also be a replica mould of an object to be cast. The patterns can be made in metal, plastic resin or wood. Allowances must be built into the cast to allow for the different characteristics of the casting material. For example, metals contract when they cool, so there must be allowance for shrinkage or distortion.

Jigs

Jigs keep material positioned in the same place whilst being machined or drilled. They can be made into a particular shape for a specific process. Jigs are used for guiding a cutting tool or drill, to ensure the hole or cut is made at the correct place every time. Jigs increase production rate, improve accuracy and reduce wastage.

A hole punch creates holes in sheets of paper.

Describe how a tool can be used in order to ensure that the holes are always cut in exactly the same place on each individual punch. [2]

A jig is commonly used[1] which is slid into the correct position for the size of sheet[1] and held against the edge of the paper[1]. The punch is then pressed to create the holes.

MARKING OUT METHODS

Marking out transfers a design or lines from a plan onto a workpiece in preparation for the next step. It provides the guidelines for cutting, bending, shaping or drilling.

Measuring and marking out should be done accurately to ensure joints or panels align correctly.

- Read dimensions from the drawing or plan correctly.
- Select an appropriate tool for the material.
- Check the markings and measurement.
- "Measure twice, cut once".

Scriber

Tool with a sharp point to scratch shallow, thin lines into metal, timbers or plastics.

Engineer's blue / layout stain

Marking blue is used in metalwork to stain a metal object. This thin layer of dye can be scratched through to reveal a bright outline of the pattern or cut line. Blue can be removed afterwards.

Marker pens, pencils, chinagraph

If the protective film is in place on polymers, a marker pen can be used. Pencil marking can be removed from timbers. Disappearing ink markers can be used on fabrics. Polymers can be marked with chinagraph which is easily rubbed off.

Marking gauge

Marking gauge uses a small pin or spur to mark wood as the tool is dragged along it. It is used to scribe a line parallel to a reference edge.

Tailor's chalk

Tailor's chalk makes a temporary marking on fabric which can be brushed or washed off. Used for marking seam allowances and for alterations.

Centre punch

Used to mark the centre point of hole for drilling. It forms enough of dimple in the metal surface to act as a guide for a drill and reduce slipping.

Pattern or tracing wheel

A pattern wheel is used to transfer the outline of a sewing pattern onto fabric.

Engineer's / combination square

For transferring angular measurements onto a workpiece and checking angles.

MATERIAL MANAGEMENT

Cut materials efficiently to minimise waste

With batch or mass production, large quantities of the same shapes will be cut from stock forms. The aim is to cut as many shapes from a sheet of material as possible to minimise waste and reduce costs.

When a shape repeats, it can be **tessellated**, which means it will fit together without gaps or overlaps. A hexagonal design is a good example of this.

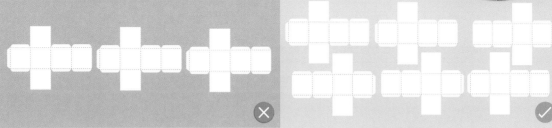

Shapes are carefully considered when set out on a material for cutting. **Nesting** lays out patterns in multiple directions with the aim to reduce material waste. Nesting profiles are often created with computer aided design for accuracy and maximum efficiency.

To calculate efficient use of material, you need to determine the amount of waste.

- Calculate the area of a sheet of material 10 cm wide × 80 cm long.
- Circular discs need to be cut from the material. Calculate the area of a disc with a diameter of 9 cm.
- Calculate the amount of waste left over from 8 discs.

Show your working. [3]

Area of the sheet 10 cm x 80 cm = 800 cm².[1] Area of the disc = πr^2
*Radius = 4.5. 3.14 x 4.5² = 63.62 cm².[1] Area of discs in cm² = 8 discs * 63.62 = 508.96 cm².[1]*
Wastage = 800 – 508.96 = 291.04 cm² of waste.[1]

Allowances

The **seam allowance** in textiles puts space between the line of stitching and the cut edge. It is important to follow the seam allowance on a pattern otherwise:

- it can affect the fit of the pattern pieces,
- it can change the way a finished garment may hang,
- it doesn't provide any allowance for fraying of the cloth and
- there will be inadequate material to press the seam open, affecting the final finish.

For a **wood joint**, the material may protrude beyond the final surface. This excess material can be removed by planing and sanding until perfectly smooth.

SPECIALIST TOOLS AND EQUIPMENT

Health and safety must be considered throughout any design process. Safe working practises are vital. If in doubt, always ask for advice or help.

Identifying and reducing risks

A **risk assessment** should be carried out before beginning work. This helps identify risks and how to minimise them. Risks should be identified for all equipment, processes and tools and logged in a risk assessment form.

Risk assessments are also required for the use of chemicals. It will identify their hazards and the precautions needed when working with chemicals.

Safety data sheets and instruction manuals

Safety data sheets provide information on safe handling and the use of chemicals. They inform those who use chemicals in the workplace to do so safely and without risk of harm to the user or the environment.

Instruction manuals contain information on the safe use of equipment and machinery.

Give **three** safety considerations when preparing a material for cutting using electric cutting tools. [3]

Care in selecting the most appropriate tool for the job so that it can be done safely.[1] Wear safety equipment such as safety glasses, dust masks or gloves.[1] Tie hair back.[1] Carry the tool with the cutting heads or attachments pointing down.[1] Ensure that you are fully trained to use the equipment before commencing the job[1], including the operation and whereabouts of the isolation switch.[1] Check the condition of the equipment and cable before use including the date of the last PAT test.[1]

Safety

To ensure personal safety
- Long hair should be tied back.
- Jewellery removed.
- Ties and any loose clothing tucked in or removed.

Personal protective equipment (PPE) must be worn at appropriate times for instance:

Working with hot metal
- Face shield
- Leather apron
- Gauntlets

Protective boots with steel toecaps

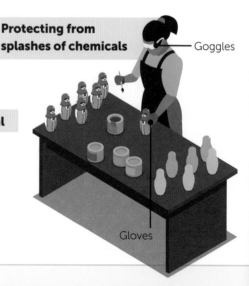

Protecting from splashes of chemicals
- Goggles
- Gloves

Working with hand tools

- Tools should be stored safely when not in use.
- Tools should be carried with sharp or cutting edges pointing downwards.
- When cutting, work should be clamped securely.

Working with machine tools

Training and guidance should be provided with all equipment. Good workshop practises include:

- Knowing how to use a machine or piece of equipment safely, including appropriate PPE.
- Knowing where the emergency stop button is situated.
- Understanding the settings and how to use safety guards.

Machinery cannot be left unattended.

Dust extraction should be used where necessary.

Work should be clamped down to minimise risk of movement.

Handling materials and waste

- When handling materials such as dyes, solvents, surface finishes and varnishes, there should be efficient ventilation.
- Avoid contact with toxic chemicals.
- Wear appropriate PPE including gloves that are protective against hazardous materials.
- Any waste chemicals should be disposed of correctly so as not to harm the environment.
- Hands should be thoroughly cleaned after working with chemicals or hazardous materials.

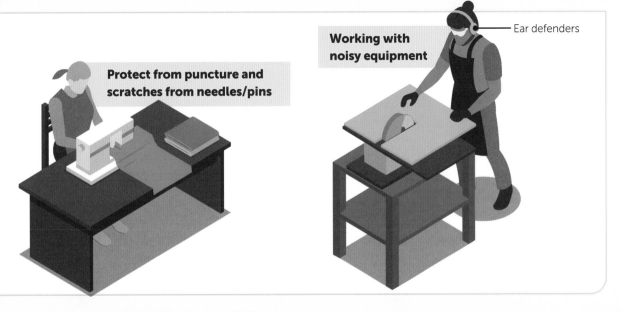

Protect from puncture and scratches from needles/pins

Working with noisy equipment

Ear defenders

SPECIALIST TECHNIQUES AND PROCESSES

In all aspects of design and manufacturing, there will be specialist tools or equipment that only perform one specific task. Specialist tools and techniques are being continually developed and it's beneficial to be aware of improvements.

Selecting the appropriate tool for the job helps achieve the required levels of accuracy and a high-quality end result.

Tools, techniques and processes are covered in each of the material sections of the book. It's always helpful to research new techniques and these can be found using:

- Internet research.
- Online videos and instruction videos on YouTube and manufacturers websites.
- Specialist discussion forums and blogs.
- Detailed instructions on the use of equipment and materials.
- Libraries and specialist magazines.

Companies and manufacturers are often willing to support school projects. Always ask permission before sending an email or telephoning.

EXAMINATION PRACTICE

1. Material availability is a key factor when choosing materials for a product.
   (a) Give **two** other factors designers need to consider when selecting materials. [2]
   (b) Discuss the impact that the availability of materials may have on a project. [6]

2. A manufacturer produces bike frames that should measure 560 mm to a tolerance of +/- 1.5 mm.
   (a) State what is meant by the term 'tolerance' with respect to quality control. [1]
   (b) Calculate the maximum and minimum height of the bike frame that would be acceptable. [2]

3. Specialist marking out tools are used when marking out a material.
   (a) Name **one** specialist marking out tool you have used. [1]
   (b) Explain how you have used the tool in part (a) with precision and accuracy. [2]

4. State what is meant by the term 'template' and explain **one** reason for using a template when marking out identical items. [3]

5. Give the name of **two** pieces of PPE that can be used to ensure your personal safety in a school workshop. [2]

6. Give **two** pieces of information that you should find out before using any new piece of equipment or machine. [2]

7. Templates, jigs and patterns can be used to ensure repetitive accuracy.

   Describe how manufacturers can use these tools to ensure batches of products are reproduced accurately. [3]

8. A stationery manufacturer is creating envelopes for greetings cards.
   Explain **one** example where tolerance may be applied. [2]

9. Discuss how material allowances and pattern or grain matching affect the costs of raw materials. [4]

10. Choose **one** product from the selection below.

Paper cup	Wooden lampstand	Metal tongs	Plastic dog chew	Textile gauntlet

   For your chosen product suggest one appropriate surface treatment or finish that could be applied to this product. [1]

EXAMINATION PRACTICE ANSWERS

1. Robots can work in hazardous environments / high temperatures / dangerous conditions, which means humans will not be exposed to these environments reducing the risk of harm / danger / personal injury.
   Factories / assembly lines can operate autonomously 24/7, which means that fewer staff are required / redundancies might have to be made / smaller workforce needed / change in job roles / reskilling / unease amongst staff. [2]

2. Reduces the distance / time / effort used to handle / move materials from section to section through production lines.
   Reduce the amount of time / distance that staff move from one section / area to another. [2]

3. Reponses may include, but are not limited to fruit / coffee / chocolate / cotton / wine. [2]

4. Internet / email / Twitter / Instagram / Facebook / YouTube. [2]

5. Oil. [1]

6. A resource in infinite supply (or in such significant abundance that we are unlikely ever to run out). [1]

7. Answers include: Rising sea levels, more frequent / more extreme weather, rising air and sea temperatures, melting of the polar ice caps. [2]

8. Waste materials can be reused to make smaller / alternative parts, which means that they buy fewer new materials. Waste materials can be sold as scrap, which means the company can recover some of the material cost. Waste can be burnt to produce heat, which means they spend less money on gas / oil to heat the building / water. [2]

9. Technology push is defined as the use / application of new scientific discoveries, which is applied to products despite their being no consumer awareness / demand driving forward innovation. Market pull is defined as products being created / designed to meet a demand; in response to consumer needs / market forces. [4]

10. 14 / (5 + 2) = 2, 2 × 5 = £10 million. [2]

11. 3D models can be generated from 2D CAD files. Drawings can be animated / fed into simulation / testing programmes. Drawings are more easily edited / revised / amended / sent electronically. Colours / textures are quickly / easily applied. CAD can be linked directly to CAM / 3D printers. [3]

12. Products are made to order, which reduces the number of products that are held in stock / money tied up.
    Products are not held in stock, which means they do not go out of date / fashion. Materials and components are only bought when required / needed, which reduces the need to hold lots of materials in stock / costing money to hold / warehouse space to hold materials. [2]

13. Old products / versions / fashions / trends become out of date / slow down with lack of software upgrade / support, which means there is a need to replace / buy new models / textiles / products which keeps profits / turnover going. Technology continues to advance / develop / improve capability, which means older products become relatively slow / no upgrades released / consumers need to upgrade / buy new versions. [2]

14. Use of specialist tools required; specialist knowledge required; outsourcing repairs can be labour intensive which is expensive; spare parts can be expensive and may need to be shipped from abroad; electrical components may be complex, or integrated into the product; materials are commonly bonded using permanent bonds rather than screws. [2]

1. Non-renewable (finite) resources will eventually run out; whereas renewable sources (non-finite) will last forever. [2]

2. (a) (2619 – 1465) / 2619, 0.4406 × 100 = 44% to the nearest whole number. [2]
   (b) (i) A process called fission which is the splitting of uranium atoms in a nuclear reactor. The process harnesses a nuclear reaction which takes place inside a reactor. This releases a large amount of energy as heat. The heat is used to generate steam which drives turbines to produce electricity. [2]
   (ii) Similarities – Both sources generate heat which boils water to create steam, which turns turbines. Differences – Nuclear generates heat through fission. Fossil fuels are burned to create heat. [2]
   (iii) The material is requires treating once it has been used. It is potentially dangerous material if it is leaked and requires expensive processing of radioactive waste. Many others do not want unsightly nuclear power stations built near them. Fears of nuclear accidents in other parts of the world cause people to be concerned about the possibility of this happening near them. [2]

3. Biomass crops require huge amounts of land; which means that less land is available / land is being turned over to grow biomass rather than food crops for human consumption. Biomass crops require lots of water; which can be a scarce commodity / can be rationed / limited in very hot summers / is in little supply in some countries. [4]

4. They are very expensive to build / set up / maintain; which takes a long time to recover the costs of the project. They can cause a great deal of environmental damage; which means that marine life can be trapped / killed. They can cause local flooding if not carefully managed; which can affect ecosystems / irrigation / local villages. [4]

5. They can be recharged / reused rather than being thrown away / sent to landfill / reduce environmental damage. They work out cheaper in the long run. The power output remains relatively stable throughout their use compared to some traditional battery types. [3]

6. (a) 5.5 × (25 /100) = 5.5 × 0.25. 1.375 kg. [2]
   (b) Metal foams have less mass compared to traditional metals; which means the overall weight of the aircraft would be less / aircraft is lighter / reduces fuel consumption. [2]

7. Protective coatings to improve weather resistance / water proofing. UV protection. Anti-bacterial agents in footwear. [2]

8. A material which reacts to an external stimulus; e.g. in the form of heat / UV light and changes / responds. [2]

9. GRP. [1]

10. (a) 125 x (4/100) = 125 x 0.04. 5 kg. [2]
    (b) Pure titanium does not react with the human body. This means it can be used without the risk of causing any harm / reaction / risk of infection to the human body. [2]

11. Answers may include: Insect repelling in clothing; when rubbed gives off / slowly releases insecticides to deter insects. Thermochromic dyes can be trapped inside fabrics; which will change colour as the body heats up / cools down. [2]

12. (a) LDR. [1]

    (b) [1]

    (c) Answers may include street lighting, solar garden lights, night lights, security lights. [2]

13. Start box, Decision box with < 125 / > 125, Correct placement of heater on, Correct placement of heater off,

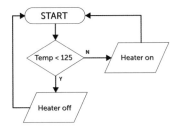

Correct placement of Yes / No, Correct feedback loops to show closed loop. [5]

14. As the input is moved 50mm to the right the output will also move to the right; and will also move 50mm. [2]

15. Pulleys and belts are more likely to slip. Belts will stretch over time and lose their grip. Belts will wear more quickly. Belts do not offer a direct drive. [2]

16. Driven / drive = 8 / 24, 8/24 = 1/3 or 1:3. [2]

1. Grams (per) Square Metre. [1]

2. Isometric grid paper / grid paper. [1]

3. Tracing paper. [1]

4. Lightweight, Impact resistant, good insulator of heat. [2]

5. Chipboard. [1]

6. Flexible, tough / shock resistant. [2]

7. It is a tough / hard material; which means it is capable of withstanding things being dropped on it / will stand up to the abrasive wear from walking on it. [2]

8. (a) Iron, carbon. [2]
   (b) Construction girders / nails / screws / car body panels. [2]

9. Copper. [1]

10. Hard, tough, electrical insulator. [2]

11. It can be moulded into thin lightweight shapes; which means it can be used to create pots / tubs / containers capable of holding food. It is a food safe material; which means it will not contaminate the yoghurt inside. [2]

12. PVC is an electrical insulator; which will prevent any chance of short circuiting between the cables / reduce the risk of electrocution / PVC is a flexible covering to allow movement of the cable. [2]

13. Cotton. [1]

14. Soft, fine, lightweight, high lustre, high strength to weight ratio. [2]

15. Fleece jackets / clothing items, backpacks, threads, sportswear. [2]

16. The ability of a material to return to its original shape; once the deforming force has been removed. [2]

1. Use sustainable materials. Source materials from local sources. Consider whether the materials can be reused / recycled at the end of the products life cycle. [3]

2. It is the FSC logo, Forest Stewardship Council; which proves that the timber has come from a sustainable source. [1]

3 Compression. [1]

4. The paper is ribbed with small wooden pieces; to add strength. The concertina folds in the paper; enable the fan to fold away. Both modifications make it stronger when fanning; without collapsing the structure of the fan. [3]

5. It is the process of bonding two or more materials together; to improve the materials strength / stability / stiffness / water resistance / durability. [2]

6. (a) It is the total number of miles a product travels; during all stages of material sourcing / processing / manufacture / though to its retail point. [2]

   (b) Mining bauxite in remote areas; bauxite is transported to a refinery; refined aluminium is sent to manufacturer; manufacturer creates cans and sends to drinks manufacturers to fill. They get sent to supermarkets or retail outlets; cans are purchased by consumers who travel back to their homes; used cans are sent for recycling (or put in landfill). [4]

7. Use green / renewable energy sources. Use more efficient machinery. Use low carbon / no carbon fuels for transportation. Make use of carbon capture / storage. [2]

8. The first 5 Rs are all chances / opportunities to do something about the materials / product / repair; whereas recycle should be the last resort if the product cannot be reused or repaired. [2]

9. Use plastic free alternatives / say 'no' to single use plastics such as straws, cups and plastic bags. Urge producers to make plastic free containers and packaging and utilise biodegradable materials, eliminate micro-beads. Reduce carbon footprint as increased greenhouse gases are making the oceans more acidic. Increase recycling to reduce waste being dumped in the oceans. [2]

10. Drilling. [1]

1. (a) List is not exhaustive. Foam board – glued / pinned / double sided tape. Cedar – glued / screwed /nailed / wood joint. Brass – screw thread / machine screws / rivets. Lycra – sewn / bonded. Acrylic – Tensol cement / screw threads. [1]

   (b) List is not exhaustive. Foam board – lightweight. Cedar – good resistance to water. Brass – malleable / good electrical conductor / easily cast. Lycra – quick drying / elastic. Acrylic – tough but brittle. [1]

2. Examples include: Paper is supplied in sheet form A3/4 for example which is easily fed into photocopiers / printers. Plywood is supplied in large flat sheets which is easily cut / machined on CNC routers to make flat pack furniture. Aluminium is available is supplied in ingots to foundries which are easily fed into a furnace for melting so that they can the material can be cast in moulds. Acrylic is available in sheet form and is easily bend / shaped on a strip heater to make leaflet / POS holders / cut / engraved on a laser. Wool is a natural spun fibre which can be knitted to make socks, jumpers and tights. [4]

3. [2]

Material and product	Way in which the material would be shaped or formed
Polyethylene terephthalate (PET) – for use in water bottles	• Extrusion is used to create the parison which is lowered into the open mould • Air is blown into the parison which forces the parison to take the shape of the mould
Foil backed board – for use in takeaway food container lids	• Foil is bonded/laminated to the board • The lids are cut / stamped out
Copper – electrical cable	• The copper is formed into a billet • The billet is pushed / drawn through a series of decreasing sized holes to make wire • Multiple wires are woven together to make stranded wire
Beech – for use as children's toys	• The tree is cut down and the timber would be cut into planks ready to be seasoned • Machining such as planing / sanding / routing would be used to shape the planks into the right sized parts
Cotton – for use as a shirt	• The cotton fibres / threads are washed / cleaned /dyed • It is then woven into the fabric from which pieces are cut
Photo sensitive printed circuit board (PCB) – for use as circuit board for a night light	• The board will be photo etched to produce the circuit image on the surface of the board • It will be drilled before components would be fixed / soldered to the board

4. (a) Batch - Handmade batches are produced on a small production line; using jigs or patterns; which enables identical products to be made to the same size / fit. [2]

   (b) Mass - Machines are set up to work for long periods; therefore, there is little down time in terms of not having machines running / products being manufactured. Volumes are high since there is a pre-determined number of products ordered / high volume to be produced. [2]

5. Any raw material such as trees / oil / wool / silk / metal ores / bauxite. [2]

6. (a) Wasting is a process that generates waste by removing material. [1]

   (b) Wasting must be appropriate to a material and may include: saw dust / filings / slithers of paper and card / cutting metal legs off components / bits of thread or other forms of unusable material generated because of cutting bits off or sanding / abrading a material. Die cutting / perforation / turning / sawing / milling / drilling / cutting / shearing. [2]

7. Offset lithography / die cutting / routing / turning / milling / casting / injection moulding / extrusion / weaving / dying / printing / pick and place assembly / flow soldering. [2]

8. Thin layers of plywood / veneers / flexi-ply can be glued together and squeezed in a former until the glue dries; to form a new shape that is stiffer / more rigid which is capable of taking more weight. Metals / papers / boards / polymers can be bent and deformed to make new shapes / hollow / creased; to increase stiffness / rigidity meaning they can stand up / support more weight / increase resistance top torsion and bending stresses. Fabric based webbing can be stuck / ironed / sewn in between fabric layers; so that shirt collars become stiffer / iron better improving its overall appearance. [2]

9. (a) Providing protection from / against the weather making the material more durable; therefore, improving the materials weather resistance / less prone to insect / fungal attack. It might provide protection against high temperatures / electricity; and prevent the risk of being burned / electrocuted. It will make the material surface harder / tougher; therefore, making it more resistant to wear / abrasion / indentation. It will make the material surface more hygienic; therefore, making it easier to clean / maintain. [2]

   (b) The surface of the material can be coloured with dyes / paints / stains; therefore, improving the materials visual appearance / appeal / makes it look nicer. Surface decorations can be applied in the form of sequins / embellishments / applique; to improve the overall appearance of the product. [2]

10. This type of response would be marked using levels based marked scheme on Page 145. The content below is indicative content and as such it is the sort of detail that would be expected to be seen. [6]

A go-no go gauge would be used to check the internal / external dimensions of the product. Micrometer would be used to check dimensions. X-rays analysis could be used to check for any cracks or hair line fractures in any welded joints. Dimensional checks would be made against the original product to ensure dimensions are identical. Stitch / sewing quality and strength would be checked on textiles garments. Fabric pattern / lay of the check pattern would be tested against a chart / original standard garment. Jigs / templates would be used to check the position and size of button holes / position of pockets / size of cuffs. Colour match tests on different batches of fabric coming into the factory. Density check on timber coming in from different trees / batches of timber. Quality / circuit flow of boards / soldering / functionality / connectivity of other parts such as screen / keyboard / CPU. Battery charger / tester to check battery storage levels. Visual inspection on polymer based products for flow marks / characteristics during any moulding processes.

11. Summer dress: Fashions change quickly therefore only a limited number of items will be needed at a time. Once made, patterns may be used many times, allowing alternative materials to be added or different colour schemes and/or prints to be added. Patterns for the item of clothing will be laid out on the material and cut in bulk at the same time. A series of workstations can be used to perform a specific task on the garment before passing it on to the next workstation. Patterns made in a range of sizes.

Cast iron cookware: Needed in relatively small numbers and will need to be made in batches to avoid overproduction. Dishes are often branded and or latest/newer versions are produced to boost sales meaning that batches are required. Designs and materials used change regularly. Pans last a long time meaning that they are not frequently replaced. Pans are cast meaning that patterns and moulds need to be produced which can be reused.

Bath toy: The toy will be rotationally moulded therefore moulds will need to be made, which lend themselves to batch production. The colours can be changed in different batches. The moulding machine can be set up with different moulds and a specific number run off before changing to an alternative mould for another product.

Pepper mill: The specific design would not be sold in high volumes therefore made in batches. The individual components would be made to a template / pattern / guide to ensure repetitive accuracy. The components would be made in a small production line. CNC lathes would be used for some of the procedures. Alterations to width and height could be easily accommodated in batch production.

Valentines card: The specific design may not be sold in high volumes therefore made in batches. Seasonal sales would suit batch production. This might be made and finished for a specific event of occasion therefore only required in small to medium numbers. Special dies with steel rules need making to cut, crease and score the card and can be used for batch production.

Christmas lights: Highly seasonal; therefore production would not need to be constant, lending itself to being batch produced. Many components would be injection moulded, needing expensive moulds to be created – they could all be used with one injection moulding machine in batches. [4]

12. (a) Award up to 2 marks for a correct answer in each of two different areas. [4]

Urea formaldehyde – for moulded electrical fittings: Easily moulded – so that it can be formed to shape. Hard – so that it can withstand knock/bumps in the home. Poor conductor so electrically insulative.

Bleed proof paper – for drawing rendered designs with marker pens: Sized surface – so that the ink from the markers pens sits on the surface / giving a deeper/richer/less faded colour / marker won't go through the paper staining the worksurface/ material underneath. Less-absorbent – good for water and spirit-based colours. Smooth surface – giving a high-quality finish.

Stainless steel – for kitchen utensils: Sheet material – available for pressed utensils. Resistant to rust – meaning that it won't corrode/rust. Hard – meaning that it will keep its shape in use. Tough – meaning it will withstand knock and bumps in use. Food safe – avoiding any contamination with food. Durable – Can withstand very high-water temperatures when being washed/sterilised. Poor conductor of heat so it is safe to hold.

Oak – for a child's toy box: Fine and dense grain – to withstand pressure exerted when used or when items are dropped/ thrown into it. Durable/resists splitting/holds paint and stains well. Tough – to withstand wear and indentation in use / resists chipping and splintering / due to a tight/even grain structure. Natural colour and grain are pleasant – attractive aesthetics when unfinished.

Cotton – for a bed sheet: Easily spun into yarn – so that it can be woven into fabric / can be blended with other fibres such as polyester for improved properties. Naturally derived insulation – so that it is warm. Breathable – to allow perspiration to pass through. Comfortable – so that the sleeper can lie against the material over a long period. Reasonably hard wearing – the sheet will last without splitting or wearing out.

Buzzer – for use in a door entry system: Compact/small – so that less space is required on PCB/in casing. Low power – meaning that battery lasts longer. Loud output – meaning that the users of the bell/alert system will notice the sound.

(b) Urea formaldehyde – oil, Bleed proof paper – trees/wood for pulp, Stainless steel – ferrite/iron ore, Oak – trees, Cotton – cotton plants, Buzzer – metal parts – copper ore / iron ore, polymer parts- oil. [1]

(c) Urea formaldehyde – fractional distillation, Bleed proof paper – wood pulp/sizing/calendering, Stainless steel – smelting in a blast furnace, Oak – timber conversion/drying/seasoning, Cotton – spinning/weaving, Buzzer – soldering/refining or fractional distillation for polymer parts/smelting or refining for copper or other metal parts. [1]

1. Interviews / questionnaires / surveys / focus Groups / case studies / user observations. [3]

2. Data may not be up to date; therefore, any designs / work based on it may not be accurate. Data is publicly available; therefore, it is not commercially sensitive if the data is being used to design a brand new / innovative product. [2]

3. It means that the product can be used by the majority of the population; which means that it will reach a huge market / improve sales / company turnover. [2]

4. The product and its purpose, The target market, who will use it, How and where it would be used, Where it would be sold, budget and timescale. [2]

5. Consumers may feel like they are doing the right thing / helping those less fortunate as fair trade ensures farmers / producers get a fair price; which means they themselves can pay their own staff / invest in their own communities / at a good level. [2]

6. **Alessi** was founded in 1921 producing metal tableware. They expanded into many household items working with industrial designers such as Rossi, Sottsass and Starck. Their products are recognisable for the use of colour, and fun design.

   Apple: An American technology company best known for bringing beauty and design to computers, iPhones and the iPod, Apple Watch and Apple TV. Their ethos of combining stylish design with a great user experience has made them the world's largest technology company, with a high level of brand loyalty.

   Braun's design was renowned for simplicity, but with a high level of user friendliness through to the smallest detail. Braun's range expanded to include shavers and other household appliances.

   Dyson made improvements to the traditional vacuum cleaner. Five years and 5,127 iterations later he developed the first bagless cleaner. High-powered motors that do not lose suction. Cordless convenience. Investment in battery technology. Dyson Ltd is now a global technology company producing household products with quality and functionality at the top of its agenda.

   Gap is a global fashion business selling their range of casual clothing in 90 countries. Denim, and their classic 5 pocket 'jean' is still at the heart of the business with a continual focus on attention to detail, comfort and design.

   Primark opened its first in Dublin in 1969 and there are now 360 stores worldwide. Their range now includes shoes, beauty products and homewares. It operates at the low-cost end of the market for shoppers seeking the latest fashions at modest prices; known as a 'fast fashion' brand.

   Under Armour was founded by Kevin Plank, an American football player who was tired of having to change of out of the sweat soaked t-shirt worn under his jersey. He developed a moisture-wicking synthetic fabric that kept athletes cool and dry. From this lightweight fabric Under Armour was born and it is now a global brand with a range of performance apparel.

   Zara was founded by Amancio Ortega in 1975 to bring catwalk high-fashion designs to everyday shoppers on tight timescales. With over 2,000 stores worldwide Zara leads in fast fashion with its highly responsive supply chain. Its efficient design, production and distribution business model enables Zara stores to receive new designs weekly. [4]

7. The process of working with others to create something; bringing people together to pool ideas and concepts, to be developed into a final solution. [2]

8. It is a form of technical drawing using international drawing conventions; which means it can be read / interpreted by an engineer in any country / fewer language barriers. It can be used to draw very large / very small products; which means dimensions can be taken from it when manufacturing products. [2]

9. To ensure the product meets the design criteria; otherwise it will not meet the original design brief / specification / market demand / need. Is fit for purpose; otherwise it might not work / fail / perform as intended. Meets all safety criteria; otherwise it will not pass any national / international standards tests. [4]

10. Graphs and charts. Simulation and predictions using computers. Data can be gathered in a spreadsheet or database and analysed. [3]

11. As the product is tested to destruction it will enable the designers to see how much force it took to break it; therefore allowing them to evaluate if it is strong enough to withstand everyday use. [2]

12. (a) 2-point perspective. [1]

    (b) (i) The science of how humans interact with objects; physically and emotionally; design for efficiency / comfort in use and in the working environment. [2]

    (ii) Width of average adult when seated / 95th percentile width for the table ends; x 2 to fit two adults widthways. Seated knee height of average adult / 95th percentile knee height; to enable a user to sit underneath the table edge. Seated elbow height; to ensure that the tabletop is at the right height for eating. [2]

1. (a) Functional needs of the product. Cost of materials. [2]
    (b) Responses may include a limited supply of materials; that may not be adequate to complete the project. Materials may not be available in the size required. Rare and hard-to-find materials may take time to obtain; and fluctuate in availability; and price; which may increase the completion time and material cost. A constant supply of raw materials may not be available; which may affect continuous or mass production.
    This question should be marked using the levels of response guidance on Page 145. [6]

2. (a) It is the amount of allowed / permitted error. [1]
    (b) Maximum = 561.5 mm and the minimum is 558.5mm. [2]

3. (a) / (b) Steel rule / tape measure / dividers / try square / engineer square / scriber / centre punch / tailors chalk / tracing wheel / sliding bevel / rotary cutting wheel.

    Make sure the tool is held firmly against the edge when using any form of square or marking out gauge; to ensure that a 90° angle is achieved.

    Mark out against the edge of a ruler; so that it will be parallel and not drift across the materials resulting in a longer / shorter dimension.

    Press firmly with the chalk / rotary cutter to ensure the pattern is marked out / cleanly cut through; so that once the pattern is removed the image will be clearly seen. [1] / [2]

4. A template is a specific shape that can be drawn or traced around. The template is a known / fixed shape which can be drawn / traced around each time; to ensure that each component is identical / reduces the risk of introducing error / having components of different sizes. [3]

5. Goggles / ear defenders / apron / gloves / face shield / mask. [2]

6. Find out where the emergency stop button is. Work out how to turn the machine / equipment on and off. Find out how / where the safety guards are / what the correct PPE is. [2]

7. Template: Easy to trace around on sheet materials, including fabric. Usually held in place using clamps, pins or clips. Template can be reprinted or reused for subsequent jobs to ensure that the shapes are identical.

    Jig: A jig is used to ensure that cutting tools flow precisely the same line or contour for every piece. The workpiece is firstly clamped to a cutting table. Some jigs are designed to hold the workpiece securely as well as to provide cutting guidelines.

    Pattern: A pattern is a relief mould used to shape flexible materials over it, such as a felt hat or vacuum formed plastic. It can also be used as a positive form to create a negative mould form, as used for casting. [3]

8. Tolerance will be applied to the measurements on a greetings card and envelope. The minimum allowable size of the envelope to allow the card to fit. [2]

9. Responses may include: Allowances require more material to be wasted or used to create seams / flush joints / printing bleed. Additional material has a direct cost. Grain matching may require that parts may not tessellate perfectly on a sheet if they are not able to rotate to have different grain directions. Cardboard sections may be punched using a die cutter may require that the corrugations all run in the same direction which may affect tessellation and increase wastage. Fabric sections of a garment may require that a stripe or pattern runs in a particular direction for each component / a pocket has the same pattern to blend in with the main fabric panel / seams align the pattern. [4]

10. Paper cup: Printing; grease proofing; wax coating. Wooden lampstand: Painting; varnishing; waxing and polishing; stain; oil. Metal tongs: Lacquer; electroplating (chrome); polishing; brushing. Plastic dog chew: Rubberising; anti-bacterial / microbial protection; polishing. Textile fire gauntlet: Dyeing; printing; decoration / embellishment; flameproofing; (Teflon®) anti-stain coating. [1]

BAND DESCRIPTIONS AND LEVELS OF RESPONSE GUIDANCE FOR EXTENDED RESPONSE QUESTIONS

Questions that require extended writing use mark bands. The whole answer will be marked together to determine which mark band it fits into and which mark should be awarded within the mark band.

Mark Band 3 **High Level 5–6 marks**	• Technical terms have been used precisely. • The answer is logical and shows an extensive understanding of Design and Technology concepts and principles. • The answer is almost always detailed and accurate. • All parts of the answer are consistent with each other. • Knowledge and ideas are applied to the context in the question • Where examples are used, they help to illustrate. • Arguments and points are developed throughout the answer with a range of different perspectives. Different sides of a discussion are considered against each other.
Mark Band 2 **Mid Level 3–4 marks**	• Technical terms used in the question have been understood. • The answer shows an understanding of D&T related concepts. • Arguments and points are developed in the answer, but sometimes useful examples or related knowledge to the context have not been included. • Some structure has been given to the answer with at least one line of reasoning. • Sound knowledge has been effectively shown.
Mark Band 1 **Low Level 1–2 marks**	• The answer shows that technical terms used in the question have not been understood. • Key concepts have not been understood and have not been related to the question context. • The answer is only loosely related to the question and some inaccuracies are present. • The answer only considers a narrow viewpoint or one angle • The answer is unstructured. • Examples used are mostly irrelevant to the question or have no evidence to support them.
0 marks	• No answer has been given or the answer given is not worth any marks.

The above descriptors have been written in simple language to give an indication of the expectations of each mark band. See the AQA website at **www.aqa.org.uk** for the official mark schemes used.

INDEX

H

hand tools 69, 135
hardening 69
hardness 30
hardwood 32, 62
Harry Beck 117
Health and Safety at Work Act
        (1974) 47
heart shaped cam 25
high carbon steel 34
high density polyethylene
        (HDPE) 36
high impact polystyrene (HIPS)
        36
high speed steel 35
hinges
    polymers 78
    timbers 66
hydroelectric power (HEP) 15
hydro-graphic printing 82

I

idler gear 26
inclusive design 8
injection moulding 80
ink jet card 31
input devices 22
instruction manuals 134
integrated circuits (IC) 102
intellectual property 4
interfacing 45
interviews 110
investigation 110
isometric projection 122
Issigonis, Alec 117
iterative design 120

J

jigs 106, 131
job roles 7
just-in-time (JIT) 9

K

Kevlar 20
kinetic energy 15, 16, 21
kinetic pumped storage systems
        16
knitted fabric 39
knock down fittings 65

L

labour 3, 47
lamination 45
    textiles 90
    timber 66
lamp 23
larch 32, 63
laser cutter 91, 130
layout paper 31
leaflets 52
lean manufacturing 9
levels of response guidance 145
levers 24
life cycle assessment (LCA)
        5, 10, 51
light dependent resistor (LDR)
        22
light emitting diode (LED) 23
linear motion 24
linen 87, 89
linkages 25
liquation 68
liquid crystal display (LCD) 17
lithography 57
    of polymers 82
Louis Comfort Tiffany 118
low carbon steel 34
lubricants 104
Lycra 38, 88

M

machine screws 71
machine tools 135
    timbers, metals, polymers 86
Mackintosh, Charles Rennie 118
magnitude 24
mahogany 32
malleability 30
man-made fibres 88
manufactured timbers 33
manufacturing methods 9
manufacturing specification 115
Marcel Breuer 117
mark allocations viii
market pull 7
market research 110, 114
market testing 121
marking out 132
Mary Quant 118
mass production 105

N

material management 133
mathematical modelling 124
McQueen, Alexander 117
measurements 106
mechanical advantage (MA) 24
mechanical devices 24
mechanism 25
medium density fibreboard
        (MDF) 33, 62
melamine formaldehyde 37
metal foam 17
metals 34, 68
microcontroller 22, 102
microfibres 21
micron 31, 53
mild steel 34
milling 73
mining 46
mixed fibres 38
modelling 121
    CAD 125
    mathematical 124
modifying plastics 76
monomer 75
Morris, William 117
motion 24
motor vehicles 98
moulding polymers 80
mouldings, timber 65
movement 24

N

nanomaterials 17
nanometre 17
natural fibres 38, 87
natural gas 13
natural timbers 32
nesting 133
non-destructive testing 121
non-ferrous metals 34
non-finite resources 5, 7, 14
non-woven textiles 39
Norman Foster 117
nuclear power 14
nuts and bolts 70
Nylon 38, 88

EXAM TIPS

With your examination practice, use a boundary approximation using the following table. Be aware that boundaries are usually a few percentage points either side of this and change each year.

Grade	9	8	7	6	5	4	3	2	1
Boundary	90%	80%	70%	60%	50%	40%	30%	20%	10%

1. Be aware of command words at the back of the specification. If 'describe' or 'explain' questions are given you need to expand your answers. To help you justify your responses, aim to include words such as BECAUSE... or SO... in every answer because this forces you to justify your point, so you get additional marks. See how well it works!

2. Explain questions such as "explain why this is the most appropriate..." do not require just a list of benefits. Instead you should identify the benefits and then expand each one, applying them to the scenario or context.

3. Full answers should be given to questions – not just key words. Make your answers match the context of the question. Where you are asked to give examples, always do so. Access to the higher marks will be difficult without examples.

4. Avoid simple one-word answers. Adjectives such as cheap, strong or quick are unlikely to gain marks unless these are justified. For example, "robots save money on wages" is not a strong answer. It would better to explain that "once the initial investment has been made, robots do not need to be paid wages but will require maintenance by more highly skilled workers".

5. Always include notes and sketches where you are asked to do so in a question. Support your drawings by using annotations and labels. Include detail such as processes and the use of any relevant tools or equipment.

6. Questions involving mathematics should be read carefully before attempting your answer. Misreading the question is a common way to lose marks on these question types. Show your working at every stage as marks can still be awarded even if the final answer is not correct.

7. Always give answers using the correct units, e.g. mm or kg, and to the correct number of decimal places.

8. In drawing questions, look out for key features such as holes or hidden detail and incorporate them into your reponses using the appropriate line styles and techniques.

9. You are required to study at least one material area. However, not all material areas provide enough scope to answer all questions that may appear in an exam, particularly with electronic and mechanical systems. For this reason, it is recommended that you study more than one material area. This gives you more knowledge and understanding to draw from and apply to a greater range of questions.

10. 15% of the marks in the paper will test mathematics skills. You can check the full maths requirements in the most up to date version of the specification. This can be downloaded from www.aqa.org.uk.

11. Attempt every question, even if you are unsure of the question or the answer. Have a go. You might just get a mark or two, but you'll be guaranteed zero marks if you don't attempt a question at all.

12. Time your practice attempts in this book and in the examination based on roughly one mark per minute. A 4-mark question should therefore be given 4 minutes to complete. The real paper is 100 marks in 120 minutes. This will allow you 1 mark per minute with 20 minutes to check through things at the end.

Good luck!